everyday
thai

This is a Parragon book
First published in 2007

Parragon
Queen Street House
4 Queen Street
Bath BA1 1HE, UK

Copyright © Parragon Books Ltd 2007
Designed by Terry Jeavons & Company

ISBN 978-1-4054-9398-7

Printed in China

This book uses metric and imperial measurements. Follow the same units of measurement throughout; do not mix metric and imperial. All spoon measurements are level, unless otherwise stated: teaspoons are assumed to be 5ml, and tablespoons are assumed to be 15ml. Unless otherwise stated, milk is assumed to be whole, eggs and individual fruits such as bananas are medium, and pepper is freshly ground black pepper.

Recipes using raw or very lightly cooked eggs should be avoided by infants, the elderly, pregnant women, convalescents, and anyone suffering from an illness. Pregnant and breast-feeding women are advised to avoid eating peanuts and peanut products.

everyday
thai

introduction

Thai cuisine has become increasingly popular in recent years, and with good reason – it's healthy, it's easy to prepare and cook and it's very distinctive in its ingredients and flavours, making a Thai meal the perfect choice for any occasion from a quick midweek supper to an elegant themed dinner party for friends.

The main problem with cooking Thai-style used to be finding the ingredients, but because we have all become so much more ambitious in the kitchen, both supermarkets and smaller specialists stores have responded and now staples such as noodles and scented Thai rice, and flavourings such as the various curry pastes,

lemon grass, chillies, galangal and coconut milk, are readily available. There are really no substitutes for these, so do make an effort to track them down – the internet is a good source of suppliers. Two exceptions are palm sugar, which is less sweet than cane or beet sugar and can be replaced with soft, light brown sugar or Indian 'jaggery', and the aniseed-flavoured Thai basil leaves, which can be replaced with common basil if you are unable to find them.

An essential piece of equipment in Thai cookery is the wok, which the Thai people use for everything – curries and soups, stir-fries and noodles, even deep-frying. A new steel wok needs seasoning before use, so wash it in warm, soapy water, scrubbing off the protective oiled coating, then rinse well and half dry. Stand the damp wok over low heat until it is completely dry, then drizzle in a little oil and wipe it around the inside of the wok with kitchen

paper. Continue to heat gently until the oil smokes and burns off, then repeat with another coating of oil. After this, the wok should never be scrubbed again, simply wiped out carefully.

Remember that every Thai meal is a relaxed and sociable event, so enjoy!

appetizers, soups & salads

This chapter is full of delicious ways to set the taste buds tingling at the start of a Thai meal. This is a concession to the Western custom of serving a separate first course, however – in Thailand, these dishes would be eaten either as snacks at any time during the day, or as appetizers before sitting down to a formal meal, or as part of the one main course, when small portions of several dishes are served on plates or in bowls and eaten together. A spoon and fork are used if, for example, a dish has a soupy consistency and includes rice or noodles, but often warm finger foods are also served which are picked up and dunked into a dipping sauce.

If you are planning to serve an authentic Thai menu, it is worth noting that soups feature in almost every Thai meal, even breakfast. Lunch is often a generous bowl of soup, a thin broth made filling and nutritious with the addition of rice or fine noodles, eggs, fish, meat or tofu, vegetables and herbs and a fresh chilli or two.

When cooking deep-fried foods, remember to pat them well with kitchen paper when you remove them from the pan to absorb any excess oil and allow the delicate flavours of the filling to be enjoyed. And serve them lukewarm, Thai-style – not only will they taste perfect, but there will be no danger of scalded mouths.

omelette rolls

ingredients

SERVES 4

4 large eggs
2 tbsp water
1 tbsp Thai soy sauce
6 spring onions, chopped
    finely
1 fresh red chilli, deseeded
    and chopped finely
1 tbsp vegetable or
    peanut oil
1 tbsp Thai green curry paste
bunch of fresh coriander,
    chopped

method

Put the eggs, water and Thai soy sauce in a bowl.
Set aside. Mix together the spring onions and chopped
chilli to form a paste.

Heat half the oil in a 20-cm/8-inch frying pan and pour
in half the egg mixture. Tilt to coat the bottom of the pan
evenly and cook until set. Lift out and set aside. Heat
the remaining oil and make a second omelette in the
same way.

Spread the spring onion and chilli paste and the curry
paste in a thin layer over each omelette and sprinkle the
coriander on top. Roll up tightly. Cut each one in half
and then cut each piece on the diagonal in half again.
Serve immediately, while still warm.

corn fritters

ingredients

SERVES 4

fritters

3 spring onions, chopped
    finely

325 g/11½ oz canned
    sweetcorn kernels, drained

1 red pepper, deseeded and
    finely chopped

small handful of fresh
    coriander, chopped

2 garlic cloves, crushed

2 eggs

2 tsp caster sugar

1 tbsp fish sauce

2 tbsp rice flour or cornflour

vegetable or peanut oil,
    for pan-frying

dip

2 red peppers, deseeded and
    halved

2 tomatoes, peeled, deseeded
    and chopped coarsely

1 tbsp vegetable or peanut oil,
    for pan-frying

1 onion, chopped

1 tbsp Thai red curry paste

3–4 sprigs fresh coriander,
    chopped

method

Combine all the ingredients for the fritters in a bowl. Heat the oil in a frying pan and cook spoonfuls of the mixture, in batches, until golden brown on the underside. Flip over with a spatula to cook the second side. Remove from the pan, drain on kitchen paper and keep warm.

To make the dip, put the red peppers on a baking sheet and place, skin-side up, under a hot grill, until blackened. Using tongs, transfer to a plastic bag, tie the top and let cool slightly.

When the peppers are cool enough to handle, peel off the skins and chop the flesh. Put into a blender or food processor with the tomatoes and process until smooth.

Heat the oil in a heavy-based saucepan and cook the onion and curry paste for 3–4 minutes, until softened. Add the pepper and tomato purée and cook gently until tender and hot. Stir in the chopped coriander, cook for 1 minute and serve hot with the fritters.

wontons

ingredients

SERVES 4

filling

2 tbsp vegetable or peanut oil

6 spring onions, chopped

125 g/4 1/2 oz mushrooms, chopped

55 g/2 oz fine green beans, chopped

55 g/2 oz sweetcorn kernels, drained if canned

1 egg, beaten

3 tbsp Thai soy sauce

1 tbsp jaggery or soft light brown sugar

1/2 tsp salt

wontons

24 wonton skins

1 egg, beaten

vegetable or peanut oil, for deep-frying

plum or chilli sauce, to serve

method

To make the filling, heat the oil in a preheated wok and stir-fry the spring onions, mushrooms and beans for 1–2 minutes, until softened. Add the corn, stir well to mix, and then push the vegetables to the side. Pour in the egg. Stir until lightly set before incorporating the vegetables and adding the soy sauce, sugar and salt. Remove the wok from the heat.

Place the wonton skins in a pile on a work surface. Put a teaspoonful of the filling in the centre of the top skin. Brush the edges with beaten egg and fold in half diagonally to make a small triangular package. Repeat with the remaining skins and filling.

Heat the oil for deep-frying in a wok or large frying pan. Add the packages, in batches, and deep-fry for 3–4 minutes, until they are golden brown. Remove from the wok with a slotted spoon and drain on kitchen paper. Keep warm while you cook the remaining wontons. Serve hot with plum or chilli sauce.

crispy egg rolls

ingredients

SERVES 4

2 tbsp vegetable or peanut oil
6 spring onions, cut into
    5-cm/2-inch lengths
1 fresh green chilli, deseeded
    and chopped
1 carrot, cut into thin sticks
1 courgette, cut into thin
    sticks
1/2 red pepper, deseeded and
    thinly sliced
115 g/4 oz beansprouts
115 g/4 oz canned bamboo
    shoots, drained and rinsed
3 tbsp Thai soy sauce
1–2 tbsp chilli sauce
8 egg roll skins
vegetable or peanut oil,
    for deep-frying

method

Heat the oil in a wok and stir-fry the spring onions and chilli for 30 seconds. Add the carrot, courgette and red pepper and stir-fry for 1 minute more. Remove the wok from the heat and stir in the beansprouts, bamboo shoots, soy sauce and chilli sauce. Taste and add more soy sauce or chilli sauce if necessary.

Place an egg roll skin on a work surface and spoon some of the vegetable mixture diagonally across the centre. Roll one corner over the filling and flip the sides of the skin over the top to enclose the filling. Continue to roll up to make an enclosed package. Repeat with the remaining skins and filling to make 8 egg rolls.

Heat the oil for deep-frying in a wok or large frying pan. Deep-fry the egg rolls, 3–4 at a time, until they are crisp and golden brown. Remove with a slotted spoon, drain on kitchen paper while you cook the remainder, then serve immediately.

lemon grass chicken skewers

ingredients

SERVES 4

2 long or 4 short lemon grass
    stems

2 large skinless, boneless
    chicken breasts, about
    400 g/14 oz in total

1 small egg white

1 carrot, finely grated

1 small fresh red chilli,
    deseeded and chopped

2 tbsp snipped fresh garlic
    chives

2 tbsp chopped coriander

salt and pepper

1 tbsp corn oil

coriander sprigs and lime
    slices, to garnish

mixed salad leaves, to serve

method

If the lemon grass stems are long, cut them in half across the centre to make 4 short lengths. Cut each stem in half lengthways, so that you have 8 sticks.

Coarsely chop the chicken pieces and place them in a food processor with the egg white. Process to a smooth paste, then add the carrot, chilli, chives, coriander and salt and pepper to taste. Process for a few seconds to mix well. Transfer the mixture to a large bowl. Cover and chill in the refrigerator for 15 minutes.

Preheat the grill to medium. Divide the mixture into 8 equal-size portions and use your hands to shape the mixture around the lemon grass 'skewers'.

Brush the skewers with oil and cook under the hot grill for 4–6 minutes, turning them occasionally, until golden brown and thoroughly cooked. Alternatively, barbecue over medium–hot coals.

Transfer to serving plates. Garnish with coriander sprigs and lime slices and serve hot with salad leaves.

chicken satay

ingredients

SERVES 4

2 tbsp vegetable or peanut oil
1 tbsp sesame oil
juice of 1/2 lime
2 skinless, boneless chicken
    breasts, cut into small
    cubes

dip

2 tbsp vegetable or peanut oil
1 small onion, chopped finely
1 small fresh green chilli,
    deseeded and chopped
1 garlic clove, chopped finely
125 ml/4 fl oz crunchy
    peanut butter
6–8 tbsp water
juice of 1/2 lime

method

Combine both the oils and the lime juice in a non-metallic dish. Add the chicken cubes, cover with clingfilm and chill for 1 hour.

To make the dip, heat the oil in a frying pan and sauté the onion, chilli and garlic over low heat, stirring occasionally, for about 5 minutes, until just softened. Add the peanut butter, water and lime juice and simmer gently, stirring constantly, until the peanut butter has softened enough to make a dip – you may need to add extra water to make a thinner consistency.

Meanwhile, drain the chicken cubes and thread them onto 8–12 wooden skewers – soak the skewers in cold water for 45 minutes before threading the meat to help stop them burning during cooking. Put under a hot grill or on a barbecue, turning frequently, for about 10 minutes, until cooked and browned. Serve hot with the warm dip.

crispy wrapped prawns

ingredients

SERVES 4

16 large, unpeeled cooked
   prawns
juice of 1 lime
4 tbsp chilli sauce
16 wonton skins
vegetable or peanut oil,
   for deep-frying
plum sauce, to serve

method

Remove the heads and shell the prawns, but leave the tails intact. Place them in a non-metallic bowl, add the lime juice, and toss lightly to coat. Set aside in a cool place for 30 minutes.

Spread a little chilli sauce over a wonton skin. Place a prawn diagonally across it, leaving the tail protruding. Fold the bottom corner of the skin over the prawn, fold the next corner up over the head end, and then roll the prawn up in the skin so that the body is encased, but the tail is exposed. Repeat with the remaining skins, chilli sauce and prawns.

Heat the oil in a wok or frying pan and deep-fry the prawns, in batches, until crisp and browned. Serve hot with plum sauce for dipping.

fish cakes

ingredients

SERVES 4

450 g/1 lb skinned white fish
   fillets, cut into cubes
1 egg white
2 kaffir lime leaves, torn
   coarsely
1 tbsp Thai green curry paste
55 g/2 oz green beans,
   chopped finely
1 fresh red chilli, deseeded
   and chopped finely
bunch of fresh coriander,
   chopped
vegetable or peanut oil for
   cooking
1 fresh green chilli, deseeded
   and sliced, to serve

dipping sauce

115 g/4 oz caster sugar
50 ml/2 fl oz white wine
   vinegar
1 small carrot, cut into thin
   sticks
5-cm/2-inch piece cucumber
   peeled, deseeded and cut
   into thin sticks

method

Put the fish into a food processor with the egg white,
lime leaves and curry paste and process until smooth.
Scrape the mixture into a bowl and stir in the green
beans, red chilli and coriander.

With dampened hands, shape the mixture into small
patties, about 5 cm/2 inches across. Place them on a
large plate in a single layer and chill for 30 minutes.

Meanwhile, make the dipping sauce. Put the sugar in
a saucepan with $1^{1}/_{2}$ tablespoons water and the vinegar
and heat gently, stirring until the sugar has dissolved.
Add the carrot and cucumber, then remove from the
heat and let cool.

Heat the oil in a frying pan and cook the fish cakes, in
batches, until golden brown on both sides. Drain on
kitchen paper and keep warm while you cook the
remaining batches.

If desired, reheat the dipping sauce. Serve the fish cakes
immediately with warm or cold dipping sauce, topped with
the green chilli slices.

beef satay with peanut sauce

ingredients

SERVES 4

500 g/1 lb 2 oz lean beef fillet,
    cut into 1-cm/1/2-inch
    cubes
2 garlic cloves, crushed
2-cm/3/4-inch piece fresh root
    ginger, finely grated
1 tbsp brown sugar
1 tbsp dark soy sauce
1 tbsp lime juice
2 tsp sesame oil
1 tsp ground coriander
1 tsp ground turmeric
1/2 tsp chilli powder
chopped cucumber and red
    pepper pieces, to garnish

peanut sauce

300 ml/10 fl oz coconut milk
8 tbsp chunky peanut butter
1/2 small onion, grated
2 tsp brown sugar
1/2 tsp chilli powder
1 tbsp dark soy sauce

method

Place the beef cubes in a large bowl. Add the garlic,
ginger, sugar, soy sauce, lime juice, sesame oil, coriander,
turmeric and chilli powder. Mix well to coat the pieces of
meat evenly. Cover and marinate in the refrigerator for at
least 2 hours or overnight.

Preheat the grill to high. To make the peanut sauce,
place all the ingredients in a small saucepan and stir
over medium heat until boiling. Remove the pan from
the heat and keep warm.

Thread the beef cubes onto presoaked bamboo skewers.
Cook the skewers under the hot grill for 3–5 minutes,
turning frequently, until golden. Alternatively, barbecue
over hot coals. Transfer to a large serving plate, then
garnish with chopped cucumber and red pepper pieces
and serve with the peanut sauce.

pork & crab meatballs

ingredients

SERVES 6

225 g/8 oz pork fillet,
    chopped finely
170 g/5¾ oz canned
    crabmeat, drained
3 spring onions, chopped
    finely
1 garlic clove, chopped finely
1 tsp Thai red curry paste
1 tbsp cornflour
1 egg white
vegetable or peanut oil,
    for deep-frying
boiled rice, to serve

sauce

1 tbsp vegetable or peanut oil
2 shallots, chopped
1 garlic clove, crushed
2 large fresh red chillies,
    deseeded and chopped
4 spring onions, chopped
3 tomatoes, chopped coarsely

method

Put the pork and crabmeat into a bowl and mix together.
Add the spring onions, garlic, curry paste, cornflour and
egg white, and beat well to make a thick paste. With
damp hands, shape the mixture into walnut-size balls.

Heat the oil in a wok and deep-fry the balls, in batches,
for 3–4 minutes, turning frequently, until golden brown
and cooked. Drain on kitchen paper and keep warm.

To make the sauce, heat the oil in a wok and stir-fry
the shallots and garlic for 1–2 minutes. Add the chillies
and spring onions and stir-fry for 1–2 minutes, then add
the tomatoes. Stir together quickly, then spoon the sauce
over the pork and crab balls. Serve immediately with rice.

vegetable & noodle soup

ingredients

SERVES 4

2 tbsp vegetable or peanut oil

1 onion, sliced

2 garlic cloves, chopped finely

1 large carrot, cut into thin sticks

1 courgette, cut into thin
    sticks

115 g/4 oz head of broccoli,
    cut into florets

1 litre/32 fl oz vegetable stock

400 ml/14 fl oz coconut milk

3–4 tbsp Thai soy sauce

2 tbsp Thai red curry paste

55 g/2 oz wide rice noodles

115 g/4 oz mung or soy
    beansprouts

4 tbsp chopped fresh
    coriander

method

Heat the oil in a wok or large frying pan and stir-fry
the onion and garlic for 2–3 minutes. Add the carrot,
courgette and broccoli and stir-fry for 3–4 minutes, until
just tender.

Pour in the stock and coconut milk and bring to the boil.
Add the soy sauce, curry paste and noodles and simmer
for 2–3 minutes, until the noodles have swelled. Stir in
the beansprouts and coriander and serve immediately.

prawn laksa

ingredients

SERVES 4

400 g/14 oz canned coconut
milk

300 ml/10 fl oz vegetable
stock

50 g/1³/₄ oz vermicelli rice
noodles

1 red pepper, deseeded and
cut into strips

225 g/8 oz canned bamboo
shoots, drained and rinsed

5-cm/2-inch piece fresh root
ginger, sliced thinly

3 spring onions, chopped

1 tbsp Thai red curry paste

2 tbsp fish sauce

1 tsp jaggery or soft light
brown sugar

6 sprigs fresh Thai basil

12 unshelled cooked prawns

method

Pour the coconut milk and stock into a saucepan and
bring slowly to the boil. Add the remaining ingredients,
except the prawns, and simmer gently for 4–5 minutes,
until the noodles are cooked.

Add the prawns and simmer for a further 1–2 minutes,
until heated through. Ladle the soup into small, warmed
bowls, dividing the prawns equally between them, and
serve immediately.

corn & crab soup

ingredients

SERVES 4

2 tbsp vegetable or peanut oil
4 garlic cloves, chopped finely
5 shallots, chopped finely
2 lemon grass stalks,
    chopped finely
2.5-cm/1-inch piece fresh
    root ginger, chopped finely
1 litre/32 fl oz chicken stock
400 g/14 oz canned coconut
    milk
225 g/8 oz frozen sweetcorn
    kernels
350 g/12 oz canned
    crabmeat, drained and
    shredded
2 tbsp fish sauce
juice of 1 lime
1 tsp jaggery or soft light
    brown sugar
bunch of fresh coriander,
    chopped, to garnish

method

Heat the oil in a large frying pan and sauté the garlic, shallots, lemon grass and ginger over low heat, stirring occasionally, for 2–3 minutes, until softened. Add the stock and coconut milk and bring to the boil. Add the corn, reduce the heat and simmer gently for 3–4 minutes.

Add the crabmeat, fish sauce, lime juice and sugar and simmer gently for 1 minute. Ladle into warmed bowls, garnish with the chopped coriander and serve at once.

spicy beef & noodle soup

ingredients

SERVES 4

1 litre/32 fl oz beef stock

150 ml/5 fl oz vegetable or
    peanut oil

85 g/3 oz rice vermicelli
    noodles

2 shallots, sliced thinly

2 garlic cloves, crushed

2.5-cm/1-inch piece fresh
    root ginger, sliced thinly

225-g/8-oz piece fillet steak,
    cut into thin strips

2 tbsp Thai green curry paste

2 tbsp Thai soy sauce

1 tbsp fish sauce

chopped fresh coriander,
    to garnish

method

Pour the stock into a large saucepan and bring to the
boil. Meanwhile, heat the oil in a wok or large frying pan.
Add a third of the noodles and cook for 10–20 seconds,
until they have puffed up. Lift out of the oil with tongs,
drain on kitchen paper and set aside. Discard all but
2 tablespoons of the oil.

Add the shallots, garlic and ginger to the wok or frying
pan and stir-fry for 1 minute. Add the beef and curry
paste and stir-fry for a further 3–4 minutes, until tender.

Add the beef mixture, the uncooked noodles, soy sauce
and fish sauce to the pan of stock simmer for 2–3
minutes, until the noodles have swelled. Serve hot,
garnished with the chopped coriander and the reserved
crispy noodles.

rice noodles with tofu soup

ingredients

SERVES 4

200 g/7 oz firm tofu, drained
vegetable or peanut oil,
    for deep-frying
1 litre/32 fl oz vegetable stock
5 spring onions, halved
1 yellow pepper, deseeded
    and sliced
2 celery stalks, sliced
1 small onion, sliced thinly
4 kaffir lime leaves
2 tbsp Thai soy sauce
1 tbsp Thai green curry paste
175 g/6 oz wide rice noodles,
    soaked and drained
chopped fresh coriander,
    to garnish

method

Using a sharp knife, cut the tofu into even cubes. Pour the oil into a wok to a depth of about 5 cm/2 inches and heat. Deep-fry the tofu, in batches, until browned all over. Remove with a slotted spoon, drain on kitchen paper and set aside.

Pour the stock into a saucepan and bring to the boil. Add the spring onions, yellow pepper, celery, onion, lime leaves, soy sauce and curry paste and simmer for 4–5 minutes. Add the noodles and the tofu and simmer for 2–3 minutes. Ladle into warmed bowls and serve hot, topped with chopped coriander.

clear soup with mushrooms & chicken

ingredients

SERVES 4

25 g/1 oz dried cèpes or other mushrooms

1 litre/32 fl oz water

2 tbsp vegetable or peanut oil

115 g/4 oz mushrooms, sliced

2 garlic cloves, chopped coarsely

5-cm/2-inch piece fresh galangal, sliced thinly

2 chicken breast portions (on the bone, skin on)

225 g/8 oz baby chestnut or white mushrooms, quartered

juice of 1/2 lime

sprigs fresh flat-leaf parsley, to garnish

method

Place the dried mushrooms in a small bowl and pour over hot water to cover. Set aside to soak for 20–30 minutes. Drain the mushrooms, reserving the soaking liquid. Cut off and discard the stalks and chop the caps coarsely.

Pour the reserved soaking water into a saucepan with the measured water and bring to the boil. Reduce the heat to a simmer.

Meanwhile, heat the oil in a wok and stir-fry the soaked mushrooms, sliced fresh mushrooms, garlic and galangal for 3–4 minutes. Add to the pan of hot water with the chicken breasts. Simmer for 10–15 minutes, until the meat comes off the bones easily.

Remove the chicken from the pan. Peel off and set aside the skin. Remove the meat from the bones, slice and set aside. Return the skin and bones to the stock and simmer for a further 30 minutes.

Remove the pan from the heat and strain the stock into a clean pan through a cheesecloth-lined sieve. Bring back to the boil and add the chestnut or white mushrooms, sliced chicken and lime juice. Reduce the heat and simmer for 8-10 minutes. Ladle into warmed bowls, garnish with parsley sprigs and serve at once.

hot-&-sour soup

ingredients

SERVES 4

6 dried shiitake mushrooms
115 g/4 oz rice vermicelli
    noodles
4 small fresh green chillies,
    deseeded and chopped
6 tbsp rice wine vinegar
850 ml/27 fl oz vegetable
    stock
2 lemon grass stalks,
    snapped in half
115 g/4 oz canned water
    chestnuts, drained, rinsed
    and halved
6 tbsp Thai soy sauce
juice of 1 lime
1 tbsp jaggery or soft light
    brown sugar
3 spring onions, chopped,
    to garnish

method

Place the dried mushrooms in a bowl and pour in
enough hot water to cover. Set aside to soak for 1 hour.
Place the noodles in another bowl and pour in enough
hot water to cover. Set aside to soak for 10 minutes.
Combine the chillies and rice wine vinegar in a third
bowl and set aside.

Drain the mushrooms and noodles. Bring the stock
to the boil in a large saucepan. Add the mushrooms,
noodles, lemon grass, water chestnuts, soy sauce, lime
juice and sugar and bring to the boil.

Stir in the chilli and vinegar mixture and cook for
1–2 minutes. Remove and discard the lemon grass.
Ladle the soup into warmed bowls and serve hot,
garnished with the spring onions.

peppered beef salad

ingredients

SERVES 4

4 x 115-g/4-oz fillet steaks

2 tbsp black peppercorns,
      crushed

1 tsp Chinese five spice powder

115 g/4 oz beansprouts

2.5-cm/1-inch piece fresh
      root ginger, chopped finely

4 shallots, sliced finely

1 red pepper, deseeded
      and sliced thinly

3 tbsp Thai soy sauce

2 fresh red chillies, deseeded
      and sliced

1/2 lemon grass stalk,
      chopped finely

3 tbsp vegetable or peanut oil

1 tbsp sesame oil

method

Wash the steaks and pat dry on kitchen paper. Mix the peppercorns with the five spice powder and press onto all sides of the steaks. Cook on a griddle pan or under a grill for 2–3 minutes each side, or until cooked to your liking.

Meanwhile mix the beansprouts, half the ginger, the shallots and pepper together and divide between 4 plates. Mix the remaining ginger, soy sauce, chillies, lemon grass and oils together.

Slice the beef and arrange on the vegetables. Drizzle with the dressing and serve immediately.

prawn &
papaya salad

ingredients

SERVES 4

1 papaya, peeled
350 g/12 oz large cooked
    prawns, shelled
assorted baby salad leaves

dressing

4 spring onions, chopped
    finely
2 fresh red chillies, deseeded
    and chopped finely
1 tsp fish sauce
1 tbsp vegetable or peanut oil
juice of 1 lime
1 tsp jaggery or soft light
    brown sugar

method

Scoop the seeds out of the papaya and slice thinly. Stir
gently together with the prawns.

Mix the spring onions, chillies, fish sauce, oil, lime juice
and sugar together.

Arrange the salad leaves in a bowl and top with the
papaya and prawns. Pour the dressing over the salad
and serve immediately.

crab & coriander salad

ingredients

SERVES 4

350 g/12 oz canned white
    crabmeat, drained
4 spring onions, finely
    chopped
handful of fresh coriander,
    chopped
1 iceberg lettuce, shredded
7.5-cm/3-inch piece
    cucumber, chopped

dressing

1 garlic clove, crushed
2.5-cm/1-inch piece fresh
    root ginger, peeled and
    grated
2 lime leaves, torn into pieces
juice of 1 lime
1 tsp fish sauce

method

Put the crabmeat into a bowl and stir in the spring
onions and coriander.

Mix the ingredients for the dressing together.

Place the lettuce leaves on a serving platter and sprinkle
with the cucumber.

Arrange the crab salad over the leaves and drizzle the
dressing over the salad. Serve immediately.

tuna & tomato salad with ginger dressing

ingredients

SERVES 4

$^1/_2$ cup shredded Napa
    cabbage
3 tbsp rice wine or dry sherry
2 tbsp Thai fish sauce
1 tbsp finely shredded fresh
    root ginger
1 garlic clove, finely chopped
$^1/_2$ small fresh red Thai chilli,
    finely chopped
2 tsp brown sugar
2 tbsp lime juice
400 g/14 oz fresh tuna steak
corn oil, for brushing
125 g/4$^1/_2$ oz cherry tomatoes
fresh mint leaves and mint
    sprigs, coarsely chopped,
    to garnish

method

Place a small pile of shredded Napa cabbage on a large serving plate. Place the rice wine or dry sherry, fish sauce, ginger, garlic, chilli, sugar and 1 tablespoon of lime juice in a screw-top jar and shake well to combine.

Using a sharp knife, cut the tuna into strips of an even thickness. Sprinkle with the remaining lime juice.

Brush a wide frying pan or ridged griddle pan with oil and heat until very hot. Arrange the tuna strips in the pan and cook until just firm and light golden, turning them over once. Remove the tuna strips from the pan and reserve.

Add the tomatoes to the pan and cook over high heat until lightly browned. Spoon the tuna and tomatoes over the Napa cabbage, then spoon over the dressing. Garnish with fresh mint and serve warm.

aubergine
& onion salad

ingredients

SERVES 4

4 tbsp vegetable or peanut oil

1 onion, sliced

4 shallots, chopped finely

4 spring onions, sliced

350 g/12 oz aubergines,
    cubed

2 tbsp Thai green curry paste

2 tbsp Thai soy sauce

1 tsp jaggery or soft light
    brown sugar

115 g/4 oz block creamed
    coconut, chopped

3 tbsp water

small handful of fresh
    coriander, chopped

few Thai basil leaves, chopped

small handful of fresh parsley,
    chopped

115 g/4 oz rocket leaves

2 tbsp sweet chilli sauce

method

Heat half the oil in a wok or large frying pan and cook all the onions together for 1–2 minutes, until just softened but not browned. Lift out and set aside.

Add the aubergine cubes, in batches if necessary, adding more oil as needed, and cook until they are crisp and golden brown.

Return the onions to the wok and add the curry paste, soy sauce and sugar. Add the creamed coconut and water and cook until dissolved. Stir in most of the coriander, the basil and the parsley.

Toss the rocket in the sweet chilli sauce and serve with the aubergine and onion salad. Garnish with the remaining herbs.

hot-&-sour vegetable salad

ingredients

SERVES 4

2 tbsp vegetable or peanut oil

1 tbsp chilli oil

1 onion, sliced

2.5-cm/1-inch piece fresh
    root ginger, grated

1 small head of broccoli, cut
    into florets

2 carrots, cut into short thin
    sticks

1 red pepper, deseeded and
    cut into squares

1 yellow pepper, deseeded
    and cut into strips

55 g/2 oz mangetout,
    trimmed and halved

55 g/2 oz baby corn, halved

dressing

2 tbsp vegetable or peanut oil

1 tsp chilli oil

1 tbsp rice wine vinegar

juice of 1 lime

1/2 tsp fish sauce

method

Heat the oils in a wok or large frying pan and sauté the
onion and ginger for 1–2 minutes until they start to
soften. Add the vegetables and stir-fry for 2–3 minutes
until they have softened slightly. Remove from the heat
and set aside.

Mix the dressing ingredients together. Transfer the
vegetables to a serving plate and drizzle the dressing
over. Serve warm immediately, or let the flavours
develop and serve cold.

curried egg salad

ingredients

SERVES 4

6 eggs

1 tbsp vegetable or peanut oil

1 onion, chopped

1 tbsp Thai yellow curry paste

4 tbsp plain yogurt

1/2 tsp salt

handful of fresh coriander,
    chopped finely

bunch of watercress or rocket

2 courgettes, cut into short
    thin sticks

1 fresh green chilli, deseeded
    and chopped finely

1 tsp fish sauce

1 tsp rice wine vinegar

3 tbsp vegetable or peanut oil

method

Put the eggs in a saucepan, cover with cold water and bring to the boil. Simmer for 10 minutes, then drain and rinse in cold water. Shell and halve.

Meanwhile, heat the oil in a medium frying pan and sauté the onion gently until softened but not browned. Remove from the heat and stir in the curry paste. Let cool slightly before stirring in the yogurt, salt and half the coriander. Set the mixture aside.

Arrange the watercress and courgettes on a platter. Mix the chilli, fish sauce, vinegar and oil together and pour the dressing over the leaves.

Arrange the eggs on top and spoon the yogurt mixture over each one. Garnish with the remaining coriander and serve immediately.

for meat lovers

The Thai Buddhist religion forbids the killing of animals, but – somewhat confusingly – not the eating of meat, which is supplied mainly by non-Buddhist butchers who are immigrants to Thailand, and is often regarded as a treat for special occasions.

Meat is cooked in a variety of ways – in curries and stir-fries, on skewers, or marinated and roasted – with wonderful seasonings that result in a dish that is hot, spicy and irresistibly tasty. Beef, pork and lamb are all served, but chicken is the most common, with duck another Thai favourite, frequently cooked under a grill with warm spices and soy or sweet glazes. Both chicken and pork are often combined with seafood such as prawns or crabmeat, and tossed with noodles, which – after rice – are Thailand's main staple. Pad Thai, a combination of rice noodles, pork and prawns, tossed together with garlic, chilli, eggs and peanuts, is the best known of all Thai noodle dishes and is the country's 'fast-food' dish.

Thai meat dishes are quick and easy to cook – curries more or less take care of themselves once the initial preparation is complete, needing only some freshly cooked rice to serve, while stir-fries are prepared, cooked and served literally in minutes, with meat, vegetables and noodles all thrown in together.

spicy beef with potato

ingredients

SERVES 4

450 g/1 lb beef fillet

2 tbsp Thai soy sauce

2 tbsp fish sauce

2 tbsp vegetable or peanut oil

3–4 coriander roots, chopped

1 tbsp crushed black
    peppercorns

2 garlic cloves, chopped

1 tbsp jaggery or soft light
    brown sugar

350 g/12 oz potatoes, diced

150 ml/5 fl oz water

bunch of spring onions,
    chopped

225 g/8 oz baby spinach
    leaves

cooked rice or noodles,
    to serve

method

Cut the beef into thick slices and place in a shallow
dish. Put the soy sauce, fish sauce, 1 tablespoon of the
oil, the coriander roots, peppercorns, garlic and sugar
in a food processor and process to a thick paste.
Scrape the paste into the dish and toss the beef to coat.
Cover with clingfilm and set aside to marinate in the
refrigerator for at least 3 hours, preferably overnight.

Heat the remaining oil in a wok. Lift the beef out of
the marinade, reserving the marinade, and cook for
3–4 minutes on each side, until browned. Add the
reserved marinade and the potatoes with the measured
water and gradually bring to the boil. Simmer for
6–8 minutes, or until the potatoes are tender.

Add the spring onions and spinach. Cook gently until the
greens have wilted. Serve immediately with rice or noodles.

mussaman curry

ingredients

SERVES 4

1 tbsp vegetable or peanut oil

450 g/1 lb beef top round, cut
    into cubes

2 tbsp Mussaman curry paste

2 large onions, cut into wedges

2 large potatoes, cut into
    chunks

400 ml/14 fl oz coconut milk

150 ml/5 fl oz water

2 cardamom pods

2 tbsp tamarind paste

2 tsp jaggery or soft light
    brown sugar

75 g/2³⁄4 oz unsalted peanuts,
    toasted or dry-fried

1 fresh red chilli, sliced thinly

boiled rice, to serve

method

Heat the oil in a wok and cook the meat, in batches,
until browned all over. Remove with a slotted spoon and
set aside.

Add the curry paste to the wok and stir-fry for 1–2 minutes.
Add the onions and potatoes and stir–fry for 4–5 minutes,
until golden brown. Remove with a slotted spoon and
set aside.

Pour the coconut milk into the wok with the measured
water and bring to the boil. Reduce the heat and simmer
for 8–10 minutes.

Return the meat and cooked vegetables to the wok.
Add the cardamom, tamarind paste and sugar and
simmer for 15–20 minutes, until the meat is tender.
Stir in the peanuts and chilli and serve with rice.

hot beef & coconut curry

ingredients

SERVES 4

400 ml/14 fl oz coconut milk

2 tbsp Thai red curry paste

2 garlic cloves, crushed

500 g/1 lb 2 oz braising steak

2 fresh kaffir lime leaves, shredded

3 tbsp lime juice

2 tbsp Thai fish sauce

1 large fresh red chilli, deseeded and sliced

1/2 tsp ground turmeric

salt and pepper

2 tbsp chopped fresh basil leaves

2 tbsp chopped coriander leaves

shredded coconut, to garnish

freshly cooked rice, to serve

method

Place the coconut milk in a large saucepan and bring to the boil. Reduce the heat and simmer gently for 10 minutes, or until it has thickened. Stir in the curry paste and garlic and simmer for a further 5 minutes.

Cut the beef into 2-cm/3/4-inch chunks. Add to the pan and bring to the boil, stirring constantly. Reduce the heat and add the kaffir lime leaves, lime juice, fish sauce, sliced chilli, turmeric and 1/2 teaspoon of salt.

Cover the pan and continue simmering for 20–25 minutes, or until the meat is tender, adding a little water if the sauce looks too dry.

Stir in the basil and coriander and season to taste with salt and pepper. Sprinkle with shredded coconut and serve with freshly cooked rice.

beef stir-fry

ingredients

SERVES 4

2 tbsp vegetable or peanut oil

2 medium red onions,
    sliced thinly

2 garlic cloves, chopped

2.5-cm/1-inch piece fresh
    root ginger, cut into thin
    sticks

2 x 115 g/4-oz beef fillets,
    sliced thinly

1 green pepper, deseeded
    and sliced

150 g/5½ oz canned bamboo
    shoots

115 g/4 oz beansprouts

2 tbsp magic paste

1 tbsp Thai red curry paste

handful of fresh coriander,
    chopped

few sprigs Thai basil

boiled rice, to serve

method

Heat the oil in a wok or large frying pan and stir-fry the
onions, garlic and ginger for 1 minute. Add the beef
strips and stir-fry over high heat until browned all over.
Add the vegetables and the two pastes and cook for
2–3 minutes until blended and cooked.

Stir in the coriander and basil and serve immediately
with boiled rice.

coconut beef curry

ingredients

SERVES 4

1 tbsp ground coriander

1 tbsp ground cumin

3 tbsp Mussaman curry paste

150 ml/5 fl oz water

75 g/2¾ oz block creamed
    coconut

450 g/1 lb beef fillet, cut into
    strips

400 ml/14 fl oz coconut milk

50 g/1¾ oz unsalted
    peanuts, chopped finely

2 tbsp fish sauce

1 tsp soft light brown sugar

4 kaffir lime leaves

boiled rice and chopped fresh
    coriander, to serve

method

Combine the coriander, cumin and curry paste in a
bowl. Pour the measured water into a saucepan, add
the creamed coconut and heat until it has dissolved.
Add the curry paste mixture and simmer for 1 minute.

Add the beef and simmer for 6–8 minutes, then add the
coconut milk, peanuts, fish sauce and sugar. Simmer
gently for 15–20 minutes, until the meat is tender.

Add the lime leaves and simmer for 1–2 minutes.
Serve the curry hot with boiled rice with chopped fresh
coriander stirred through it.

beef with fresh noodles

ingredients

SERVES 4

6 dried black cloud Chinese
    mushrooms
2 tbsp vegetable or peanut oil
2 x 225-g/8-oz sirloin steaks,
    sliced thickly
1 onion, cut into thin wedges
2 garlic cloves, chopped
1 green pepper, deseeded
    and chopped
3 celery stalks, sliced
2 tbsp Thai green curry paste
300 ml/10 fl oz beef stock
4 tbsp black bean sauce
225 g/8 oz fresh egg noodles
4 tbsp chopped fresh parsley

method

Put the mushrooms in a bowl, cover with boiling water and set aside to soak for 30 minutes. Drain and break up any larger pieces.

Heat the oil in a wok and stir-fry the steak over high heat until browned. Add the mushrooms, onion, garlic, pepper and celery and stir-fry for 3–4 minutes. Add the curry paste, beef stock and black bean sauce and stir-fry for 2–3 minutes.

Meanwhile, cook the noodles in boiling water for 3–4 minutes, drain well, and stir into the wok. Sprinkle the parsley over and stir. Serve immediately.

red-hot beef with cashew nuts

ingredients

SERVES 4

500 g/1 lb 2 oz lean boneless
  beef sirloin
1 tsp vegetable oil

marinade

1 tbsp sesame seeds
1 garlic clove, chopped
1 tbsp finely chopped fresh
  root ginger
1 fresh red Thai chilli,
  chopped
2 tbsp dark soy sauce
1 tsp Thai red curry paste

to finish

1 tsp sesame oil
4 tbsp unsalted cashew nuts
1 spring onion, thickly sliced
  diagonally
cucumber slices, to garnish

method

Using a sharp knife, cut the beef into 1-cm/^{1}/$_2$-inch wide strips. Place them in a large, non-metallic bowl.

To make the marinade, toast the sesame seeds in a heavy-based frying pan over medium heat for 2–3 minutes, or until golden brown, shaking the pan occasionally.

Place the seeds in a mortar with the garlic, ginger and chilli and, using a pestle, grind to a smooth paste. Add the soy sauce and curry paste and mix well.

Spoon the paste over the beef strips and toss to coat the meat evenly. Cover and marinate in the refrigerator for at least 2–3 hours or overnight.

Heat a heavy-based frying pan or ridged griddle pan until very hot and brush with vegetable oil. Place the beef strips in the pan and cook quickly, turning frequently, until lightly browned. Remove the pan from the heat and spoon the beef into a pile on a hot serving dish.

Heat the sesame oil in a small frying pan. Add the cashew nuts and quickly cook until golden. Add the spring onion and stir-fry for 30 seconds. Sprinkle the mixture on top of the beef strips, then garnish with cucumber slices and serve immediately.

beef with onions & broccoli

ingredients

SERVES 4

2 tbsp vegetable or peanut oil

2 tbsp Thai green curry paste

2 x 175-g/6-oz sirloin steaks,
   sliced thinly

2 onions, sliced

6 spring onions, chopped

2 shallots, chopped finely

225 g/8 oz head of broccoli,
   cut into florets

400 ml/14 fl oz coconut milk

3 kaffir lime leaves, chopped
   coarsely

4 tbsp chopped fresh
   coriander

few Thai basil leaves

method

Heat the oil in a wok and stir-fry the curry paste for
1–2 minutes. Add the meat, in batches if necessary,
and stir-fry until starting to brown.

Add the onions, spring onions and shallots and stir-fry
for 2–3 minutes. Add the broccoli and stir-fry for a further
2–3 minutes.

Pour in the coconut milk, add the lime leaves and bring
to the boil. Simmer gently for 8–10 minutes, until the
meat is tender. Stir in the chopped coriander and basil
leaves and serve immediately.

stir-fried beef with beansprouts

ingredients

SERVES 4

1 bunch of spring onions

2 tbsp corn oil

1 garlic clove, crushed

1 tsp finely chopped fresh
    root ginger

500 g/1 lb 2 oz lean beef
    fillet, cut into thin strips

1 large red pepper, deseeded
    and sliced

1 small fresh red chilli,
    deseeded and chopped

225 g/8 oz fresh beansprouts

1 small lemon grass stem,
    finely chopped

2 tbsp smooth peanut butter

4 tbsp coconut milk

1 tbsp rice vinegar or white
    wine vinegar

1 tbsp soy sauce

1 tsp brown sugar

250 g/9 oz medium egg
    noodles

salt and pepper

method

Thinly slice the spring onions, reserving some slices to use as a garnish.

Heat the oil in a frying pan or preheated wok over high heat. Add the spring onions, garlic and ginger and stir-fry for 2–3 minutes to soften. Add the beef and continue stir-frying for 4–5 minutes, or until evenly browned.

Add the pepper and stir-fry for a further 3–4 minutes. Add the chilli and beansprouts and stir-fry for 2 minutes. Mix the lemon grass, peanut butter, coconut milk, vinegar, soy sauce and sugar together in a bowl, then stir into the pan.

Meanwhile, cook the egg noodles in boiling salted water for 4 minutes, or according to the packet directions. Drain and stir into the pan, tossing to mix evenly.

Season to taste with salt and pepper. Sprinkle with the reserved spring onions and serve hot.

grilled beef salad

ingredients

SERVES 4

50 g/1³/₄ oz dried oyster
    mushrooms
600 g/1 lb 5 oz rump steak
1 red pepper, deseeded and
    thinly sliced
55 g/2 oz roasted cashew
    nuts
red and green lettuce leaves
fresh mint leaves, to garnish

dressing

2 tbsp sesame oil
2 tbsp Thai fish sauce
2 tbsp sweet sherry
2 tbsp oyster sauce
1 tbsp lime juice
1 fresh red chilli, deseeded
    and finely chopped

method

Put the mushrooms in a heatproof bowl, cover with boiling water and let stand for 20 minutes. Drain, then cut into slices.

Preheat the grill to medium or heat a ridged griddle pan. To make the dressing, place all the ingredients in a bowl and whisk to combine.

Cook the steak under the preheated grill or on the hot griddle pan, turning once, for 5 minutes, or until browned on both sides but still rare in the centre. Cook the steak longer if desired.

Slice the steak into thin strips and place in a bowl with the mushrooms, pepper and nuts. Add the dressing and toss together.

Arrange the lettuce on a large serving platter and place the beef mixture on top. Garnish with mint leaves. Serve at room temperature.

red lamb curry

ingredients

SERVES 4

2 tbsp vegetable oil

1 large onion, sliced

2 garlic cloves, crushed

500 g/1 lb 2 oz lean boneless
leg of lamb, cut into 3-cm/
1¼ -inch cubes

2 tbsp Thai red curry paste

150 ml/5 fl oz coconut milk

1 tbsp brown sugar

1 large red pepper, deseeded
and thickly sliced

150 ml/5 fl oz lamb or beef
stock

1 tbsp Thai fish sauce

2 tbsp lime juice

225 g/8 oz canned water
chestnuts, drained

2 tbsp chopped coriander

2 tbsp chopped fresh basil

salt and pepper

fresh basil leaves, to garnish

freshly cooked jasmine rice,
to serve

method

Heat the oil in a large frying pan or preheated wok over high heat. Add the onion and garlic and stir-fry for 2–3 minutes to soften. Add the meat and stir-fry the mixture quickly until lightly browned.

Stir in the curry paste and cook for a few seconds, then add the coconut milk and sugar and bring to the boil. Reduce the heat and simmer for 15 minutes, stirring occasionally.

Stir in the pepper, stock, fish sauce and lime juice, then cover and simmer for a further 15 minutes, or until the meat is tender.

Add the water chestnuts, coriander and basil and season to taste with salt and pepper. Transfer to serving plates, then garnish with basil leaves and serve with jasmine rice.

lamb with lime leaves

ingredients

SERVES 4

2 fresh red Thai chillies

2 tbsp peanut oil

2 garlic cloves, crushed

4 shallots, chopped

2 lemon grass stems, sliced

6 fresh kaffir lime leaves

1 tbsp tamarind paste

2 tbsp palm sugar

450 g/1 lb lean boneless
    lamb (leg or loin fillet)

300 ml/10 fl oz coconut milk

175 g/6 oz cherry tomatoes,
    halved

1 tbsp chopped coriander

freshly cooked Thai fragrant
    rice, to serve

method

Using a sharp knife, deseed and very finely chop the
chillies. Reserve until required.

Heat the oil in a large, preheated wok. Add the garlic,
shallots, lemon grass, lime leaves, tamarind paste, sugar
and chillies to the wok and stir-fry for 2 minutes.

Using a sharp knife, cut the lamb into thin strips or cubes.

Add the lamb to the wok and stir-fry for 5 minutes,
tossing well so that the lamb is evenly coated in the
spice mixture.

Pour the coconut milk into the wok and bring to the boil.
Reduce the heat and simmer for 20 minutes.

Add the cherry tomatoes and chopped coriander to the
wok and simmer for 5 minutes. Transfer to serving
plates and serve hot with fragrant rice.

stir-fried lamb with mint

ingredients

SERVES 4

2 tbsp vegetable oil

2 garlic cloves, finely sliced

2 fresh red chillies, deseeded
and cut into thin strips

1 onion, thinly sliced

1½ tbsp Madras curry paste

500 g/1 lb 2 oz lamb fillet,
cut into thin strips

225 g/8 oz canned baby corn
cobs, drained

4 spring onions, finely
chopped

55 g/2 oz fresh mint leaves,
coarsely shredded

1 tbsp Thai fish sauce

freshly cooked rice, to serve

method

Heat half the oil in a preheated wok or large frying pan.
Add the garlic and chillies and cook until soft. Remove
and reserve. Add the onion and cook for 5 minutes, or
until soft. Remove and reserve.

Heat the remaining oil in the wok. Add the curry paste
and cook for 1 minute. Add the lamb, in batches if
necessary, and cook for 5–8 minutes, or until cooked
through and tender.

Return the onion to the wok with the baby corn cobs,
spring onions, mint and fish sauce. Cook until heated
through. Sprinkle the garlic and chillies over and serve
with rice.

red curry pork
with peppers

ingredients

SERVES 4

2 tbsp vegetable or peanut oil

1 onion, coarsely chopped

2 garlic cloves, chopped

450 g/1 lb pork fillet, sliced
    thickly

1 red pepper, deseeded and
    cut into squares

175 g/6 oz mushrooms,
    quartered

2 tbsp Thai red curry paste

115 g/4 oz block creamed
    coconut, chopped

300 ml/10 fl oz pork or
    vegetable stock

2 tbsp Thai soy sauce

4 tomatoes, peeled, deseeded
    and chopped

handful of fresh coriander,
    chopped

boiled noodles or rice,
    to serve

method

Heat the oil in a wok or large frying pan and sauté the
onion and garlic for 1–2 minutes, until they are softened
but not browned.

Add the pork slices and stir-fry for 2–3 minutes until
browned all over. Add the pepper, mushrooms and
curry paste.

Dissolve the coconut in the hot stock and add to the wok
with the soy sauce. Bring to the boil and simmer for 4–5
minutes until the liquid has reduced and thickened.

Add the tomatoes and coriander and cook for
1–2 minutes before serving with noodles or rice.

pad thai

ingredients

SERVES 4

225 g/8 oz thick rice-stick
   noodles

2 tbsp vegetable or peanut oil

2 garlic cloves, chopped

2 fresh red chillies, deseeded
   and chopped

175 g/6 oz pork fillet, sliced
   thinly

115 g/4 oz uncooked prawns,
   shelled and chopped

8 fresh Chinese chives,
   chopped

2 tbsp fish sauce

juice of 1 lime

2 tsp jaggery or soft light
   brown sugar

2 eggs, beaten

115 g/4 oz beansprouts

4 tbsp chopped fresh
   coriander

115 g/4 oz unsalted peanuts,
   chopped, plus extra to
   serve

crispy fried onions, to serve

method

Soak the noodles in warm water for 10 minutes, drain
well and set aside.

Heat the oil in a wok and stir-fry the garlic, chillies and
pork for 2–3 minutes. Add the prawns and stir-fry for a
further 2–3 minutes.

Add the chives and noodles, then cover and cook for
1–2 minutes. Add the fish sauce, lime juice, sugar
and eggs. Cook, stirring and tossing constantly to mix
in the eggs.

Stir in the beansprouts, coriander and peanuts and
serve with small dishes of crispy fried onions and extra
chopped peanuts.

spicy fried minced pork

ingredients

SERVES 4

2 tbsp corn oil

2 garlic cloves, finely chopped

3 shallots, finely chopped

2.5-cm/1-inch piece fresh root ginger, finely chopped

500 g/1 lb 2 oz minced lean pork

2 tbsp Thai fish sauce

1 tbsp dark soy sauce

1 tbsp Thai red curry paste

4 dried kaffir lime leaves, crumbled

4 plum tomatoes, chopped

3 tbsp chopped coriander

salt and pepper

freshly cooked fine egg noodles, to serve

coriander sprigs and spring onion tassels, to garnish

method

Heat the oil in a large frying pan or preheated wok over medium heat. Add the garlic, shallots and ginger and stir-fry for 2 minutes. Stir in the pork and continue stir-frying until golden brown.

Stir in the fish sauce, soy sauce, curry paste and lime leaves and stir-fry for a further 1–2 minutes over high heat.

Add the chopped tomatoes and cook for a further 5–6 minutes, stirring occasionally. Stir in the chopped coriander and season to taste with salt and pepper.

Serve hot, spooned onto freshly cooked fine egg noodles, garnished with coriander sprigs and spring onion tassels.

pork with vegetables

ingredients

SERVES 4

8 tbsp vegetable or peanut oil

115 g/4 oz rice vermicelli
    noodles

4 belly pork strips, sliced
    thickly

1 red onion, sliced

2 garlic cloves, chopped

2.5-cm/1-inch piece fresh
    root ginger, sliced thinly

1 large fresh red chilli,
    deseeded and chopped

115 g/4 oz baby corn, halved
    lengthways

1 red pepper, deseeded and
    sliced

175 g/6 oz head of broccoli,
    cut into florets

150 g/5½ oz jar black bean
    sauce

115 g/4 oz beansprouts

method

Heat the oil in a wok and cook the rice noodles, in batches,
for 15–20 seconds, until they puff up. Remove with a
slotted spoon, drain on kitchen paper and set aside.

Pour off all but 2 tablespoons of the oil and stir-fry the
pork, onion, garlic, ginger and chilli for 4–5 minutes, or
until the meat has browned.

Add the corn, red pepper and broccoli and stir-fry for
3–4 minutes, until the vegetables are just tender. Stir in
the black bean sauce and beansprouts, then cook for a
further 2–3 minutes. Serve immediately, topped with the
crispy noodles.

pork with mixed green beans

ingredients

SERVES 4

2 tbsp vegetable or peanut oil

2 shallots, chopped

225 g/8 oz pork fillet, sliced thinly

2.5-cm/1-inch piece fresh galangal, sliced thinly

2 garlic cloves, chopped

300 ml/10 fl oz chicken stock

4 tbsp chilli sauce

1 tbsp crunchy peanut butter

115 g/4 oz fine green beans

115 g/4 oz frozen broad beans

115 g/4 oz string beans, sliced

crispy noodles, to serve

method

Heat the oil in a wok and stir-fry the shallots, pork, galangal and garlic until lightly browned.

Add the chicken stock, chilli sauce and peanut butter and stir until the peanut butter has melted. Add all the beans and simmer for 3–4 minutes. Serve hot with crispy noodles.

pork with peppers

ingredients

SERVES 4

1 tbsp vegetable or peanut oil

1 tbsp chilli oil

450 g/1 lb pork fillet, sliced
thinly

2 tbsp green chilli sauce

6 spring onions, sliced

2.5-cm/1-inch piece fresh
root ginger, sliced thinly

1 red pepper, deseeded and
sliced

1 yellow pepper, deseeded
and sliced

1 orange pepper, deseeded
and sliced

1 tbsp fish sauce

2 tbsp Thai soy sauce

juice of $1/2$ lime

4 tbsp chopped fresh parsley

cooked flat rice noodles,
to serve

method

Heat both the oils in a wok. Add the pork, in batches,
and stir-fry until browned all over. Remove with a slotted
spoon and set aside.

Add the chilli sauce, spring onions and ginger to the
wok and stir-fry for 1–2 minutes. Add the peppers and
stir-fry for 2–3 minutes.

Return the meat to the wok, stir well, and add the fish
sauce, soy sauce and lime juice. Cook for a further 1–2
minutes, then stir in the chopped parsley and serve with
flat rice noodles.

chicken & peanut curry

ingredients

SERVES 4

1 tbsp vegetable or peanut oil

2 red onions, sliced

2 tbsp Penang curry paste

400 ml/14 fl oz coconut milk

150 ml/5 fl oz chicken stock

4 kaffir lime leaves, torn
coarsely

1 lemon grass stalk, chopped
finely

6 skinless, boneless chicken
thighs, chopped

1 tbsp fish sauce

2 tbsp Thai soy sauce

1 tsp jaggery or soft, light
brown sugar

50 g/1¾ oz unsalted
peanuts, roasted and
chopped, plus extra to
garnish

175 g/6 oz fresh pineapple,
chopped coarsely

15-cm/6-inch piece cucumber,
peeled, deseeded and
sliced thickly, plus extra
to garnish

method

Heat the oil in a wok and stir-fry the onions for 1 minute.
Add the curry paste and stir-fry for 1–2 minutes.

Pour in the coconut milk and stock. Add the lime leaves
and lemon grass and simmer for 1 minute. Add the
chicken and gradually bring to the boil. Simmer for
8–10 minutes, until the chicken is tender.

Stir in the fish sauce, soy sauce and sugar and simmer
for 1–2 minutes. Stir in the peanuts, pineapple and
cucumber and cook for 30 seconds. Serve immediately,
sprinkled with extra nuts and cucumber.

green chicken curry

ingredients

SERVES 4

1 tbsp vegetable or peanut oil

1 onion, sliced

1 garlic clove, chopped finely

2–3 tbsp Thai green curry
paste

400 ml/14 fl oz coconut milk

150 ml/5 fl oz chicken stock

4 kaffir lime leaves

4 skinless, boneless chicken
breasts, cut into cubes

1 tbsp fish sauce

2 tbsp Thai soy sauce

grated rind and juice of 1/2 lime

1 tsp jaggery or soft light
brown sugar

4 tbsp chopped fresh
coriander, to garnish

method

Heat the oil in a wok or large frying pan and stir-fry the
onion and garlic for 1–2 minutes, until starting to soften.
Add the curry paste and stir-fry for 1–2 minutes.

Add the coconut milk, stock and lime leaves, bring to
the boil and add the chicken. Reduce the heat and
simmer gently for 15–20 minutes, until the chicken is
tender.

Add the fish sauce, soy sauce, lime rind and juice and
sugar. Cook for 2–3 minutes, until the sugar has dissolved.
Serve immediately, garnished with chopped coriander.

chicken with yellow curry sauce

ingredients

SERVES 4

spice paste

6 tbsp Thai yellow curry paste

150 ml/5 fl oz plain yogurt

400 ml/14 fl oz water

handful of fresh coriander,
    chopped

handful of fresh Thai basil
    leaves, shredded

stir-fry

2 tbsp vegetable or peanut oil

2 onions, cut into thin wedges

2 garlic cloves, chopped finely

2 skinless, boneless chicken
    breasts, cut into strips

175 g/6 oz baby corn, halved
    lengthways

to garnish

chopped fresh coriander

shredded fresh basil

method

To make the spice paste, stir-fry the yellow curry paste in a wok for 2–3 minutes, then stir in the yogurt, water and herbs. Bring to the boil, then simmer for 2–3 minutes.

Meanwhile, heat the oil in a wok and stir-fry the onions and garlic for 2–3 minutes. Add the chicken and corn and stir-fry for 3–4 minutes, until the meat and corn are tender.

Stir in the spice paste and bring to the boil. Simmer for 2–3 minutes, until heated through. Serve immediately, garnished with extra herbs.

minced chicken skewers

ingredients

SERVES 4

450 g/1 lb minced chicken

1 onion, chopped finely

1 fresh red chilli, deseeded
and chopped

2 tbsp Thai red curry paste

1 tsp jaggery or soft light
brown sugar

1 tsp ground coriander

1 tsp ground cumin

1 egg white

8 lemon grass stalks

boiled rice with chopped
spring onion, to serve

method

Combine the chicken, onion, chilli, curry paste and sugar in a bowl and stir well to make a thick paste. Stir in the ground coriander, cumin and egg white and mix again.

Divide the mixture into 8 equal portions and squeeze them around each of the lemon grass stalks. Arrange on a griddle pan and cook under high heat, turning frequently, until browned and cooked through. Serve hot with the rice with the spring onion stirred through it.

gingered chicken kebabs

ingredients

SERVES 4

3 skinless, boneless chicken
  breasts, cut into cubes
juice of 1 lime
2.5-cm/1-inch piece fresh
  root ginger, peeled and
  chopped
1 fresh red chilli, deseeded
  and sliced
2 tbsp vegetable or peanut oil
1 onion, sliced
2 garlic cloves, chopped
1 aubergine, cut into chunks
2 courgettes, cut into thick
  slices
1 red pepper, deseeded and
  cut into squares
2 tbsp Thai red curry paste
2 tbsp Thai soy sauce
1 tsp jaggery or soft light
  brown sugar
boiled rice, with chopped
  fresh coriander, to serve

method

Put the chicken cubes in a shallow, non-metallic dish.
Mix the lime, ginger and chilli together and pour over
the chicken pieces. Stir gently to coat. Cover and chill
for at least 3 hours to marinate.

Thread the chicken pieces onto soaked wooden skewers
and cook under a hot grill for 3–4 minutes, turning
often, until cooked through.

Meanwhile, heat the oil in a wok or large frying pan and
sauté the onion and garlic for 1–2 minutes, until softened
but not browned. Add the aubergine, courgettes and
pepper and cook for 3–4 minutes, until cooked but still
firm. Add the curry paste, soy sauce and sugar and
cook for 1 minute.

Serve the vegetables and kebabs hot with boiled rice,
stirred through with chopped coriander.

spiced coriander chicken

ingredients

SERVES 4

4 skinless, boneless chicken
　　breasts
2 garlic cloves
1 fresh green chilli, deseeded
2-cm/³/₄-inch piece fresh root
　　ginger
4 tbsp chopped coriander
finely grated rind of 1 lime
3 tbsp lime juice
2 tbsp light soy sauce
1 tbsp caster sugar
170 ml6 fl oz coconut milk

to garnish

finely chopped coriander
cucumber slices
radish slices
¹/₂ fresh red chilli, deseeded
　　and sliced into rings
freshly cooked rice, to serve

method

Using a sharp knife, cut 3 deep slashes into the skinned side of each chicken breast. Place the breasts in a single layer in a non-metallic dish.

Place the garlic, chilli, ginger, coriander, lime rind and juice, soy sauce, sugar and coconut milk in a food processor and process to a smooth paste.

Spread the paste over both sides of the chicken breasts, coating them evenly. Cover with clingfilm and marinate in the refrigerator for 1 hour.

Preheat the grill to medium. Lift the chicken from the marinade, then drain off the excess and place on a grill pan. Cook under the hot grill for 12–15 minutes, or until thoroughly and evenly cooked.

Meanwhile, place the remaining marinade in a saucepan and bring to the boil. Reduce the heat and simmer for several minutes. Transfer the chicken breasts to serving plates. Garnish with chopped coriander, cucumber slices, radish slices and chilli rings and serve with rice.

chicken with vegetables & coriander rice

ingredients

SERVES 4

3 tbsp vegetable or peanut oil

2 red onions, 1 chopped and 1 sliced

2 garlic cloves, chopped

2.5-cm/1-inch piece fresh root ginger, peeled and chopped

2 skinless, boneless chicken breasts, cut into strips

115 g/4 oz white mushrooms

400 ml/14 oz canned coconut milk

55 g/2 oz sugar snap peas

2 tbsp Thai soy sauce

1 tbsp fish sauce

350 g/12 oz rice, cooked and cooled

8 oz/250 g pak choi, torn into large pieces

handful of fresh coriander, chopped

method

Heat 2 tablespoons of the oil in a wok or large frying pan and sauté the chopped onion, garlic and ginger together for 1–2 minutes.

Add the chicken and mushrooms and cook over high heat until browned. Add the coconut milk, sugar snap peas, 2 tablespoons of the soy sauce and the fish sauce and bring to the boil. Simmer gently for 4–5 minutes until tender.

Meanwhile, heat the remaining oil in a separate wok or large frying pan and cook the sliced onion until softened but not browned.

Add the cooked rice, pak choi and fresh coriander and heat through gently until the leaves have wilted and the rice is hot. Sprinkle over the remaining soy sauce and serve immediately with the chicken.

egg-fried rice with chicken

ingredients

SERVES 4

225 g/8 oz jasmine rice

3 skinless, boneless chicken
    breasts, cut into cubes

400 ml/14 fl oz canned
    coconut milk

50 g/1¾ oz block creamed
    coconut, chopped

2–3 coriander roots, chopped

thinly pared rind of 1 lemon

1 fresh green chilli, deseeded
    and chopped

3 fresh Thai basil leaves

1 tbsp fish sauce

1 tbsp oil

3 eggs, beaten

fresh chives and fresh
    coriander sprigs,
    to garnish

method

Cook the rice in boiling water for 12–15 minutes, drain well, then let cool and chill overnight.

Put the chicken into a saucepan and cover with the coconut milk. Add the creamed coconut, coriander roots, lemon rind and chilli and bring to the boil. Simmer for 8–10 minutes, until the chicken is tender. Remove from the heat. Stir in the basil and fish sauce.

Meanwhile, heat the oil in a wok and stir-fry the rice for 2–3 minutes. Pour in the eggs and stir until they have cooked and mixed with the rice. Line 4 small ovenproof bowls or ramekins with clingfilm and pack with the rice. Turn out carefully onto serving plates and remove the clingfilm. Garnish with long chives and sprigs of coriander. Serve with the chicken.

ginger chicken with noodles

ingredients

SERVES 4

2 tbsp vegetable or peanut oil

1 onion, sliced

2 garlic cloves, chopped finely

5-cm/2-inch piece fresh root
ginger, sliced thinly

2 carrots, sliced thinly

4 skinless, boneless chicken
breasts, cut into cubes

300 ml/10 fl oz chicken stock

4 tbsp Thai soy sauce

225 g/8 oz canned bamboo
shoots, drained and rinsed

75 g/2¾ oz flat rice noodles

4 spring onions, chopped,
and 4 tbsp chopped fresh
coriander, to garnish

method

Heat the oil in a wok and stir-fry the onion, garlic, ginger and carrots for 1–2 minutes, until softened. Add the chicken and stir-fry for 3–4 minutes, until the chicken is cooked through and lightly browned.

Add the stock, soy sauce and bamboo shoots and gradually bring to the boil. Simmer for 2–3 minutes. Meanwhile, soak the noodles in boiling water for 6–8 minutes. Drain well, then garnish with the spring onions and coriander and serve immediately, with the chicken stir-fry.

gingered chicken & vegetable salad

ingredients

SERVES 4

4 skinless, boneless chicken
    breasts
4 spring onions, chopped
2.5-cm/1-inch piece fresh
    root ginger, chopped finely
4 garlic cloves, 2 crushed and
    2 chopped
3 tbsp vegetable or peanut oil
1 onion, sliced
2 garlic cloves, chopped
115 g/4 oz baby corn, halved
115 g/4 oz mangetout, halved
    lengthways
1 red pepper, deseeded and
    sliced
7.5-cm/3-inch piece
    cucumber, peeled,
    deseeded and sliced
4 tbsp Thai soy sauce
1 tbsp soft light brown sugar
few Thai basil leaves
175 g/6 oz fine egg noodles

method

Cut the chicken into large cubes, each about 2.5 cm/
1 inch. Mix the spring onions, ginger, crushed garlic and
2 tablespoons of the oil together in a shallow dish
and add the chicken. Cover and marinate for at least
3 hours. Lift the meat out of the marinade and set aside.

Heat the remaining oil in a wok or large frying pan and
cook the onion for 1–2 minutes. Add the garlic, baby
corn, mangetout and pepper and cook for 2–3 minutes,
until just tender. Add the cucumber, half the soy sauce,
the sugar and the basil and mix gently.

Soak the noodles for 2–3 minutes (check the packet
instructions) or until tender, and drain well. Sprinkle the
remaining soy sauce over them and arrange on plates.
Top with the cooked vegetables.

Add a little more oil to the wok if necessary and cook the
chicken over fairly high heat until browned on all sides.
Arrange the chicken cubes on top of the salad and serve
hot or warm.

red chicken salad

ingredients

SERVES 4

4 boneless chicken breasts

2 tbsp Thai red curry paste

2 tbsp vegetable or peanut oil

1 head Napa cabbage,
    shredded

175 g/6 oz pak choi, torn into
    large pieces

1/2 savoy cabbage, shredded

2 shallots, chopped finely

2 garlic cloves, crushed

1 tbsp rice wine vinegar

2 tbsp sweet chilli sauce

2 tbsp Thai soy sauce

method

Slash the flesh of the chicken several times and rub the curry paste into each cut. Cover and chill overnight.

Cook in a heavy-based frying pan over medium heat or on a griddle pan for 5-6 minutes, turning once or twice, until cooked through. Keep warm.

Heat 1 tablespoon of the oil in a wok or large frying pan and stir-fry the Napa cabbage, pak choi and savoy cabbage until just wilted. Add the remaining oil, shallots and garlic and stir-fry until just tender but not browned. Add the vinegar, chilli sauce and soy sauce. Remove from the heat.

Arrange the leaves on 4 serving plates. Slice the chicken, arrange on the salad leaves and drizzle the hot dressing over. Serve immediately.

duck breasts with chilli & lime

ingredients

SERVES 4

4 boneless duck breasts
2 garlic cloves, crushed
4 tsp brown sugar
3 tbsp lime juice
1 tbsp soy sauce
1 tsp chilli sauce
1 tsp vegetable oil
2 tbsp plum jam
150 ml/5 fl oz chicken stock
salt and pepper
freshly cooked rice and crisp
    salad leaves, to serve

method

Using a small, sharp knife, cut deep slashes in the skin of the duck to make a diamond pattern. Place the duck breasts in a wide, non-metallic dish.

Mix the garlic, sugar, lime juice, soy sauce and chilli sauce together in a bowl, then spoon over the duck breasts, turning well to coat evenly. Cover and marinate in the refrigerator for at least 3 hours or overnight.

Drain the duck, reserving the marinade. Heat a large, heavy-based frying pan until very hot and brush with the oil. Add the duck breasts, skin-side down, and cook for 5 minutes, or until the skin is browned and crisp. Tip away the excess fat. Turn the duck breasts over.

Continue cooking on the other side for 2–3 minutes to brown. Add the reserved marinade, plum jam and stock and simmer for 2 minutes. Season to taste with salt and pepper. Transfer to individual serving plates, then spoon over the pan juices and serve hot with freshly cooked rice and crisp salad leaves.

duck salad

ingredients

SERVES 4

4 boneless duck breasts,
   skin on
1 lemon grass stalk, broken
   into three and each cut in
   half lengthways
3 tbsp vegetable or peanut oil
2 tbsp sesame oil
1 tsp fish sauce
1 fresh green chilli, deseeded
   and chopped
2 tbsp Thai red curry paste
1/2 fresh pineapple, peeled
   and sliced
7.5-cm/3-inch piece
   cucumber, peeled,
   deseeded and sliced
3 tomatoes, cut into wedges
1 onion, sliced thinly

dressing

juice of 1 lemon
2 garlic cloves, crushed
1 tsp jaggery
2 tbsp vegetable or peanut oil

method

Unwrap the duck and let the skin dry out overnight in
the refrigerator.

The following day, slash the skin side 5 or 6 times. Mix
the lemon grass, 2 tablespoons of the vegetable oil, all
the sesame oil, fish sauce, chilli and curry paste together
in a shallow dish and place the duck breasts in the
mixture. Turn to coat and to rub the marinade into the
meat. Chill for 2–3 hours.

Heat the remaining oil in a wok or large frying pan and
cook the duck, skin-side down, over medium heat for 3–4
minutes until the skin is browned and crisp and the meat
cooked most of the way through.

Turn the breasts over and cook until browned and the
meat is cooked to your liking.

Meanwhile, arrange the pineapple, cucumber, tomatoes,
and onions on a platter. Mix the dressing ingredients
together and pour over the top.

Lift the duck out of the wok and slice thickly. Arrange the
duck slices on top of the salad and serve while still hot.

for seafood fans

With Thailand's miles of coastline and many inland waterways, it is hardly surprising that the Thais are primarily a fish-eating nation. The warm tropical seas bring an abundance of fish and shellfish, while even the channels between the paddy fields are teeming with many types of fish.

In Thai coastal towns, there are rows of thatch-roofed beach kiosks selling fresh seafood from the warm Gulf waters – everything imaginable, from grilled or sautéed fish with ginger to prawns in coconut and coriander, is there to tempt both locals and visitors alike. Even in the heart of Bangkok city, the street markets are packed with fresh fish and seafood.

Like meat, fish and seafood are quickly transformed into delicious curries, stir-fries and salads, and steaming in a traditional bamboo steamer is also a very popular method of cooking fish. Thick, meaty chunks of monkfish, cod or salmon can be left for an hour or two in a refreshing chilli and lime marinade, and hold their shape and texture perfectly as they are cooked. Creamy coconut milk features in many Thai dishes – it blends particularly well with the kick of Thai spices to create curry sauces with a delicate flavour that is perfect for fish.

mixed seafood curry

ingredients

SERVES 4

1 tbsp vegetable or peanut oil

3 shallots, chopped finely

2.5-cm/1-inch piece fresh
    galangal, peeled and
    sliced thinly

2 garlic cloves, chopped finely

400 ml/14 fl oz canned
    coconut milk

2 lemon grass stalks,
    snapped in half

4 tbsp fish sauce

2 tbsp chilli sauce

225 g/8 oz uncooked jumbo
    prawns, shelled

225 g/8 oz baby squid,
    cleaned and sliced thickly

225 g/8 oz skinned salmon
    fillet, cut into chunks

175 g/6 oz tuna steak, cut
    into chunks

225 g/8 oz fresh mussels,
    scrubbed and debearded

fresh Chinese chives, to garnish

boiled rice, to serve

method

Heat the oil in a large wok and stir-fry the shallots, galangal and garlic for 1–2 minutes, until they start to soften. Add the coconut milk, lemon grass, fish sauce and chilli sauce. Bring to the boil, reduce the heat and simmer for 1–2 minutes.

Add the prawns, squid, salmon and tuna and simmer for 3–4 minutes, until the prawns have turned pink and the fish is cooked.

Add the mussels and cover with a lid. Simmer for 1–2 minutes, until they have opened. Discard any mussels that remain closed. Garnish with Chinese chives and serve immediately with rice.

fish curry

ingredients

SERVES 4

juice of 1 lime

4 tbsp fish sauce

2 tbsp Thai soy sauce

1 fresh red chilli, deseeded
and chopped

350 g/12 oz monkfish fillet,
cut into cubes

350 g/12 oz salmon fillets,
skinned and cut into
cubes

400 ml/14 fl oz coconut milk

3 kaffir lime leaves

1 tbsp Thai red curry paste

1 lemon grass stalk (white
part only), chopped finely

225 g/8 oz jasmine rice,
boiled

4 tbsp chopped fresh
coriander

method

Combine the lime juice, half the fish sauce and the soy
sauce in a shallow, non-metallic dish. Add the chilli and
the fish, stir to coat, cover with clingfilm and chill for
1–2 hours, or overnight.

Bring the coconut milk to the boil in a saucepan and
add the lime leaves, curry paste, the remaining fish
sauce and the lemon grass. Simmer gently for
10–15 minutes.

Add the fish and the marinade and simmer for
4–5 minutes, until the fish is cooked. Serve hot with
boiled rice with chopped coriander stirred through it.

fish curry with rice noodles

ingredients

SERVES 4

2 tbsp vegetable or peanut oil

1 large onion, chopped

2 garlic cloves, chopped

75 g/3 oz white mushrooms

225 g/8 oz monkfish, cut into
cubes, each about
2.5 cm/1 inch

225 g/8 oz salmon fillets, cut
into cubes, each about
2.5 cm/1 inch

225 g/8 oz cod, cut into
cubes, each about
2.5 cm/1 inch

2 tbsp Thai red curry paste

400 g/14 oz canned coconut
milk

handful of fresh coriander,
chopped

1 tsp soft light brown sugar

1 tsp fish sauce

115 g/4 oz rice noodles

3 spring onions, chopped

55 g/2 oz beansprouts

few Thai basil leaves

method

Heat the oil in a wok or large frying pan and gently
sauté the onion, garlic and mushrooms until softened
but not browned.

Add the fish, curry paste and coconut milk and bring
gently to the boil. Simmer for 2–3 minutes, then add half
the coriander, the sugar and fish sauce. Keep warm.

Meanwhile, soak the noodles for 3–4 minutes (check
the packet instructions) or until tender, and drain well
through a colander. Put the colander and noodles over
a pan of simmering water. Add the spring onions,
beansprouts and most of the basil and steam on top of
the noodles for 1–2 minutes or until just wilted.

Pile the noodles onto warmed serving plates and top
with the fish curry. Sprinkle the remaining coriander and
basil over the top and serve immediately.

stir-fried rice noodles with marinated fish

ingredients

SERVES 4

450 g/1 lb monkfish or cod, cubed

225 g/8 oz salmon fillets, cubed

2 tbsp vegetable or peanut oil

2 fresh green chillies, deseeded and chopped

grated rind and juice of 1 lime

1 tbsp fish sauce

115 g/4 oz wide rice noodles

2 tbsp vegetable or peanut oil

2 shallots, sliced

2 garlic cloves, chopped finely

1 fresh red chilli, deseeded and chopped

2 tbsp Thai soy sauce

2 tbsp chilli sauce

method

Place the fish in a shallow, non-metallic bowl. To make the marinade, mix the oil, green chillies, lime juice and rind and fish sauce together and pour over the fish. Cover and chill for 2 hours.

Put the noodles in a bowl and cover with boiling water. Leave for 8–10 minutes (check the packet instructions) and drain well.

Heat the oil in a wok or large frying pan and sauté the shallots, garlic and red chilli until lightly browned. Add the soy sauce and chilli sauce. Add the fish and the marinade to the wok and stir-fry gently for 2–3 minutes until cooked through.

Add the drained noodles and stir gently. Sprinkle with coriander and serve immediately.

rice with seafood & squid

ingredients

SERVES 4

2 tbsp vegetable or peanut oil

3 shallots, chopped finely

2 garlic cloves, chopped finely

225 g/8 oz jasmine rice

300 ml/10 fl oz fish stock

4 spring onions, chopped

2 tbsp Thai red curry paste

225 g/8 oz baby squid,
    cleaned and sliced thickly

225 g/8 oz white fish fillets,
    skinned and cut into
    cubes

225 g/8 oz salmon fillets,
    skinned and cut into
    cubes

4 tbsp chopped fresh
    coriander

method

Heat 1 tablespoon of the oil in a wok and stir-fry the shallots and garlic for 2–3 minutes, until softened. Add the rice and stir-fry for 2–3 minutes.

Add a ladleful of the stock and simmer, adding more stock as needed, for 12–15 minutes, until tender. Transfer to a dish, let cool and chill overnight.

Heat the remaining oil in a wok and stir-fry the spring onions and curry paste for 2–3 minutes. Add the squid and fish and stir-fry gently to avoid breaking up the fish. Stir in the rice and coriander, heat through gently and serve.

fish in coconut

ingredients

SERVES 4

2 tbsp vegetable or peanut oil
6 spring onions, chopped
    coarsely
2.5-cm/1-inch piece fresh
    root ginger, grated
2–3 tbsp Thai red curry paste
400 ml/14 fl oz coconut milk
150 ml/5 fl oz fish stock
4 kaffir lime leaves
1 lemon grass stalk, halved
350 g/12 oz skinned white fish
    fillets, cut into chunks
225 g/8 oz squid rings and
    tentacles
225 g/8 oz large cooked
    shelled prawns
1 tbsp fish sauce
2 tbsp Thai soy sauce
4 tbsp chopped fresh Chinese
    chives
boiled jasmine rice with
    chopped fresh coriander,
    to serve

method

Heat the oil in a wok or large frying pan and stir-fry the spring onions and ginger for 1–2 minutes. Add the curry paste and stir-fry for 1–2 minutes.

Add the coconut milk, fish stock, lime leaves and lemon grass. Bring to the boil, then reduce the heat and simmer for 1 minute.

Add the fish, squid and prawns and simmer for 2–3 minutes, until the fish is cooked. Add the fish and soy sauces and stir in the chives. Serve immediately with jasmine rice with fresh coriander stirred through it.

spiced steamed fish

ingredients

SERVES 4–6

2.5-cm/1-inch piece fresh
    root ginger, finely grated

1 lemon grass stem (base
    only), thinly sliced

6 fresh red chillies, deseeded
    and coarsely chopped

1 small red onion, finely
    chopped

1 tbsp Thai fish sauce

900 g/2 lb whole fish, cleaned

2 fresh kaffir lime leaves,
    thinly sliced

2 fresh basil sprigs

freshly cooked rice and thin
    cucumber sticks, to serve

method

Place the ginger, lemon grass, chillies, onion and fish
sauce in a food processor. Process to a coarse paste,
adding a little water, if needed.

Cut 3–4 deep slits crosswise on each side of the fish.
Spread over the spice paste, rubbing it well into the slits.
Place the fish in a dish deep enough to hold the liquid
that collects during steaming. Sprinkle over the lime
leaves and basil.

Set up a steamer or place a rack into a wok or deep
frying pan. Bring about 5 cm/2 inches of water to the
boil in the steamer or wok.

Place the dish of fish into the steamer or on the rack.
Reduce the heat to a simmer, then cover tightly and
steam the fish for 15–20 minutes, or until cooked through.
Serve with freshly cooked rice and cucumber sticks.

steamed yellow fish fillets

ingredients

SERVES 4

500 g/1 lb 2 oz firm fish fillets,
    such as red snapper, sole
    or monkfish
1 red bird chilli
1 small onion, chopped
3 garlic cloves, chopped
2 coriander sprigs
1 tsp coriander seeds
1/2 tsp ground turmeric
1/2 tsp pepper
1 tbsp Thai fish sauce
2 tbsp coconut milk
1 small egg, beaten
2 tbsp rice flour
fresh red and green chilli
    strips, to garnish
stir-fried vegetables, to serve

method

Using a sharp knife, remove any skin from the fish and cut the fillets diagonally into 2-cm/³/₄-inch wide strips.

Place the bird chilli, onion, garlic, coriander and coriander seeds in a mortar and, using a pestle, grind to make a smooth paste.

Transfer the paste to a bowl and add the turmeric, pepper, fish sauce, coconut milk and beaten egg, stirring to mix evenly. Spread the rice flour out on a large plate. Dip the fish strips into the paste mixture, then into the rice flour to coat lightly.

Bring the water in the bottom of a steamer to the boil, then arrange the fish strips in the top of the steamer. Cover and steam for 12–15 minutes, or until the fish is just firm.

Garnish the fish with the chilli strips and serve immediately with stir-fried vegetables.

pan-fried
spiced salmon

ingredients

SERVES 4

2.5-cm/1-inch piece fresh
    root ginger, grated

1 tsp coriander seeds, crushed

$^1/_4$ tsp chilli powder

1 tbsp lime juice

1 tsp sesame oil

4 salmon fillet pieces with skin,
    about 150 g/5$^1/_2$ oz each

2 tbsp vegetable oil

stir-fried vegetables and
    freshly cooked rice,
    to serve

coriander leaves, to garnish

method

Mix the ginger, crushed coriander, chilli powder, lime juice and sesame oil together in a bowl.

Place the salmon on a wide, non-metallic plate or dish and spoon the mixture over the flesh side of the fillets, spreading it to coat each piece of salmon evenly.

Cover the dish with clingfilm and chill in the refrigerator for 30 minutes.

Heat a wide, heavy-based frying pan or ridged griddle pan with the vegetable oil over high heat. Place the salmon in the hot pan, skin-side down, and cook for 4–5 minutes, without turning, until the salmon is crusty underneath and the flesh flakes easily.

Serve the salmon immediately, with stir-fried vegetables and freshly cooked rice garnished with coriander leaves.

salmon with red curry in banana leaves

ingredients

SERVES 4

4 salmon steaks, about
    175 g/6 oz each
2 banana leaves, halved
1 garlic clove, crushed
1 tsp grated fresh root ginger
1 tbsp Thai red curry paste
1 tsp brown sugar
1 tbsp Thai fish sauce
2 tbsp lime juice

to garnish

lime wedges
whole fresh red chillies
finely chopped fresh red chilli

method

Place a salmon steak in the centre of each half banana leaf. Mix the garlic, ginger, curry paste, sugar and fish sauce together, then spread over the surface of the fish. Sprinkle with lime juice.

Carefully wrap the banana leaves around the fish, tucking in the sides as you go to make neat, compact pockets.

Place the pockets seam-side down on a baking sheet. Bake in a preheated oven, 220°C/425°F/Gas Mark 7, for 15–20 minutes, or until the fish is cooked and the banana leaves are beginning to brown.

Serve garnished with lime wedges, whole chillies and finely chopped chilli.

monkfish with lime and chilli sauce

ingredients

SERVES 4

4 x 115-g/4-oz monkfish
   fillets

25 g/1 oz rice flour or
   cornflour

6 tbsp vegetable or peanut oil

4 garlic cloves, crushed

2 large fresh red chillies,
   deseeded and sliced

2 tsp jaggery or soft light
   brown sugar

juice of 2 limes

grated rind of 1 lime

boiled rice, to serve

method

Toss the fish in the flour, shaking off any excess. Heat the oil in a wok and cook the fish on all sides until browned and cooked through, taking care when turning not to break it up.

Lift the fish out of the wok and keep warm. Add the garlic and chillies and stir-fry for 1–2 minutes, until they have softened.

Add the sugar, the lime juice and rind and 2–3 tablespoons of water and bring to the boil. Simmer gently for 1–2 minutes, then spoon the mixture over the fish. Serve immediately with rice.

spiced tuna in sweet-&-sour sauce

ingredients

SERVES 4

4 fresh tuna steaks, about
    500 g/1 lb 2 oz in total

1/4 tsp pepper

2 tbsp peanut oil

1 onion, diced

1 small red pepper, deseeded
    and cut into short thin
    sticks

1 garlic clove, crushed

1/2 cucumber, deseeded and
    cut into short thin sticks

2 pineapple slices, diced

1 tsp finely chopped fresh
    root ginger

1 tbsp brown sugar

1 tbsp cornflour

1 1/2 tbsp lime juice

1 tbsp Thai fish sauce

300 ml/10 fl oz fish stock

lime slices and cucumber
    slices, to garnish

method

Sprinkle the tuna steaks with pepper on both sides.
Heat a heavy-based frying pan or ridged griddle pan
and brush with a little of the oil. Arrange the tuna steaks
in the pan and cook for 8 minutes, turning them once.

Meanwhile, heat the remaining oil in a separate frying
pan. Add the onion, pepper and garlic and cook gently
for 3–4 minutes to soften.

Remove the pan from the heat and stir in the cucumber,
pineapple, ginger and sugar.

Blend the cornflour with the lime juice and fish sauce,
then stir into the stock and add to the pan. Stir over
medium heat until boiling, then cook for 1–2 minutes,
or until thickened and clear.

Spoon the sauce over the tuna and serve immediately,
garnished with slices of lime and cucumber.

baked cod with a curry crust

ingredients

SERVES 4

1/2 tsp sesame oil

4 cod fillet pieces, about
    150 g/5 1/2 oz each

175 g/6 oz fresh white
    breadcrumbs

2 tbsp blanched almonds,
    chopped

2 tsp Thai green curry paste

finely grated rind of 1/2 lime,
    plus extra thinly pared rind
    to garnish

salt and pepper

lime slices, to garnish

boiled new potatoes and
    mixed salad leaves,
    to serve

method

Brush the oil over the bottom of a wide, shallow ovenproof dish or pan, then arrange the cod pieces in a single layer.

Mix the breadcrumbs, almonds, curry paste and grated lime rind together in a bowl, stirring well to blend thoroughly and evenly. Season to taste with salt and pepper.

Carefully spoon the crumb mixture over the fish pieces, pressing lightly with your hand to hold it in place.

Bake the dish, uncovered, in a preheated oven, 200°C/400°F/Gas Mark 6, for 35–40 minutes, or until the fish is cooked through and the crumb topping is golden brown.

Serve the dish hot, garnished with lime slices and rind and accompanied by boiled new potatoes and mixed salad leaves.

sea bass & mango salad

ingredients

SERVES 2

2 small sea bass, cleaned

1 tbsp Thai red curry paste

small handful of fresh
    coriander, chopped

150 ml/5 fl oz coconut milk

2 tbsp sweet chilli sauce

6-8 Thai basil leaves, chopped

$^1/_2$ tsp fish sauce

1 tsp rice wine vinegar

1 mango, deseeded, peeled
    and sliced

selection of mixed salad leaves

method

Place the fish on a board. Mix the curry paste and coriander together and stuff inside each fish cavity. Cover and marinate for 1–2 hours.

Place the fish in a roasting pan. Mix the coconut milk, chilli sauce, basil, fish sauce and vinegar and pour over the fish. Arrange the mango slices in the pan as well. Cover with foil and cook in a preheated oven, 200°C/400°F/Gas Mark 6, for 15 minutes.

Remove the foil and cook uncovered for a further 10–15 minutes, until cooked.

Place the fish on 2 warmed serving plates, drizzle with the cooking sauces and serve with the mixed salad leaves.

stir-fried squid with hot black bean sauce

ingredients

SERVES 4

750 g/1 lb 10 oz squid,
    cleaned and tentacles
    discarded

1 large red pepper, deseeded

115 g/4 oz mangetout

1 head pak choi

3 tbsp black bean sauce

1 tbsp Thai fish sauce

1 tbsp rice wine or dry sherry

1 tbsp dark soy sauce

1 tsp brown sugar

1 tsp cornflour

1 tbsp water

1 tbsp corn oil

1 tsp sesame oil

1 small fresh red Thai chilli,
    chopped

1 garlic clove, finely chopped

1 tsp grated fresh root ginger

2 spring onions, chopped

method

Cut the squid body cavities into quarters lengthways.
Use the tip of a small, sharp knife to score a diamond
pattern into the flesh, without cutting all the way through.
Pat dry with kitchen paper.

Cut the pepper into long, thin slices. Cut the mangetout
in half diagonally. Coarsely shred the pak choi.

Mix the black bean sauce, fish sauce, rice wine, soy sauce
and sugar together in a bowl. Blend the cornflour with the
water and stir into the other sauce ingredients. Reserve
until required.

Heat the oils in a preheated wok. Add the chilli, garlic,
ginger and spring onions and stir-fry for 1 minute. Add
the pepper slices and stir-fry for 2 minutes.

Add the squid and stir-fry over high heat for a further
1 minute. Stir in the mangetout and pak choi and stir for
a further 1 minute, or until wilted.

Stir in the sauce ingredients and cook, stirring constantly,
for 2 minutes, or until the sauce thickens and clears.
Serve immediately.

squid &
red peppers

ingredients

SERVES 4

spice paste

2 tbsp vegetable or peanut oil

1 tbsp chilli oil with prawns

2 shallots, chopped

2–3 large fresh red chillies,
deseeded and chopped

2 tbsp ground coriander

2 tbsp ground cumin

2.5-cm/1-inch piece fresh
root ginger, chopped

1 tbsp finely chopped lemon
grass

3–4 coriander roots, chopped

1 tsp salt

1 tsp soft light brown sugar

stir-fry

2 red peppers, deseeded and
diced

150 ml/5 fl oz plain yogurt

750 g/1 lb 10 oz squid,
cleaned and sliced

juice of 1 lime

115 g/4 oz block creamed
coconut, chopped

150 ml/5 fl oz hot water

method

Put all the ingredients for the spice paste into a food processor and process until chopped finely.

Scrape the spice paste into a wok and stir-fry gently for 3–4 minutes. Add the red peppers and stir-fry for 1–2 minutes.

Add the yogurt and bring to the boil. Add the squid and simmer for 2–3 minutes, then stir in the lime juice, coconut and water. Simmer for a further 1–2 minutes, until the coconut dissolves. Serve immediately.

spicy scallops with lime & chilli

ingredients

SERVES 4

16 large scallops, shelled
1 tbsp butter
1 tbsp vegetable oil
1 tsp crushed garlic
1 tsp grated fresh root ginger
1 bunch of spring onions,
    finely sliced
finely grated rind of 1 lime
1 small fresh red chilli,
    deseeded and very finely
    chopped
3 tbsp lime juice
lime wedges, to garnish
freshly cooked rice, to serve

method

Using a sharp knife, trim the scallops to remove any black intestine, then wash and pat dry with kitchen paper. Separate the corals from the white parts, then slice each white part in half horizontally, making 2 circles.

Heat the butter and oil in a frying pan or preheated wok. Add the garlic and ginger and stir-fry for 1 minute without browning. Add the spring onions and stir-fry for a further 1 minute.

Add the scallops and continue stir-frying over high heat for 4–5 minutes. Stir in the lime rind, chilli and lime juice and cook for a further 1 minute.

Transfer the scallops to serving plates, then spoon over the pan juices and garnish with lime wedges. Serve hot with freshly cooked rice.

curried noodles with prawns & straw mushrooms

ingredients

SERVES 4

1 tbsp vegetable or peanut oil

3 shallots, chopped

1 fresh red chilli, deseeded
   and chopped

1 tbsp Thai red curry paste

1 lemon grass stalk (white
   part only), chopped finely

225 g/8 oz cooked shelled
   prawns

400 g/14 oz canned straw
   mushrooms, drained

2 tbsp fish sauce

2 tbsp Thai soy sauce

225 g/8 oz fresh egg noodles

fresh coriander, chopped,
   to garnish

method

Heat the oil in a wok and stir-fry the shallots and chilli
for 2–3 minutes. Add the curry paste and lemon grass
and stir-fry for 2–3 minutes.

Add the prawns, mushrooms, fish sauce and soy sauce
and stir well to mix.

Meanwhile, cook the noodles in boiling water for
3–4 minutes, drain and transfer to warmed plates.
Top with the prawn curry, sprinkle the coriander over
and serve immediately.

prawn & pineapple curry

ingredients

SERVES 4

1/2 fresh pineapple

400 ml/14 fl oz coconut
    cream

2 tbsp Thai red curry paste

2 tbsp fish sauce

2 tsp sugar

350 g/12 oz raw jumbo
    prawns

2 tbsp chopped coriander

steamed jasmine rice, to serve

method

Peel the pineapple and chop the flesh. Heat the coconut cream, pineapple, curry paste, fish sauce and sugar in a wok or saucepan until almost boiling.

Shell and devein the prawns. Add the prawns and chopped coriander to the wok and simmer for 3 minutes, or until the prawns are cooked – they are cooked when they have turned a bright pink colour.

Serve the prawns with steamed jasmine rice.

noodles with prawns & green peppers

ingredients

SERVES 4

250 g/9 oz rice noodles

1 tbsp vegetable oil

2 garlic cloves, crushed

1 fresh red chilli, deseeded and thinly sliced

1 green pepper, deseeded and thinly sliced

6 spring onions, coarsely chopped

2 tsp cornflour

2 tbsp oyster sauce

1 tbsp Thai fish sauce

1 tsp sugar

300 ml/10 fl oz chicken stock

250 g/9 oz small cooked prawns, shelled

method

Prepare the noodles according to the packet directions. Drain, then rinse under cold water and drain again.

Heat the oil in a preheated wok. Add the garlic, chilli, pepper and spring onions. Cook for 1 minute, then transfer to a plate and reserve.

Blend the cornflour with a little water and add to the wok with the oyster sauce, fish sauce, sugar and stock. Stir over medium heat until the mixture boils and thickens.

Return the pepper and spring onion mixture to the wok with the prawns and noodles. Cook, stirring, for 2 minutes, or until heated through. Transfer to a heated serving bowl and serve immediately.

prawns with noodles

ingredients

SERVES 4

450 g/1 lb uncooked jumbo
  prawns
1 tbsp vegetable or peanut oil
3 shallots, chopped finely
2 garlic cloves, chopped finely
2.5-cm/1-inch piece fresh
  root ginger, sliced thinly
400 ml/14 fl oz canned
  coconut milk
1 tbsp Thai green curry paste
3–4 fresh Thai basil leaves
1 tsp jaggery or soft light
  brown sugar
225 g/8 oz flat rice noodles
2 tsp sesame oil
2 tbsp sesame seeds, toasted
sprigs fresh Thai basil,
  to garnish

method

Remove and discard the heads and shell the prawns.
Cut a slit along the back of each and remove and
discard the dark vein.

Heat the oil in a wok and stir-fry the shallots, garlic and
ginger for 2–3 minutes. Add the coconut milk and curry
paste and simmer for 2–3 minutes.

Add the prawns, basil leaves and sugar and cook until
the prawns turn pink.

Meanwhile, cook the noodles in boiling water according
to the packet instructions, then drain well. Stir in the
sesame oil and seeds, garnish with the sprigs of basil
and serve immediately with the prawns.

prawns with coconut rice

ingredients

SERVES 4

115 g/4 oz dried Chinese
    mushrooms
2 tbsp vegetable or peanut oil
6 spring onions, chopped
55 g/2 oz dry unsweetened
    coconut
1 fresh green chilli, deseeded
    and chopped
225 g/8 oz jasmine rice
150 ml/5 fl oz fish stock
400 ml/14 fl oz coconut milk
350 g/12 oz cooked shelled
    prawns
6 sprigs fresh Thai basil

method

Place the mushrooms in a small bowl, cover with hot water and set aside to soak for 30 minutes. Drain, then cut off and discard the stalks and slice the caps.

Heat 1 tablespoon of the oil in a wok and stir-fry the spring onions, coconut and chilli for 2–3 minutes, until lightly browned. Add the mushrooms and stir-fry for 3–4 minutes.

Add the rice and stir-fry for 2–3 minutes, then add the stock and bring to the boil. Reduce the heat and add the coconut milk. Simmer for 10–15 minutes, until the rice is tender. Stir in the prawns and basil, heat through and serve.

prawns with spring onions & straw mushrooms

ingredients

SERVES 4

2 tbsp vegetable or peanut oil
bunch of spring onions,
  chopped
2 garlic cloves, chopped finely
175 g/6 oz block creamed
  coconut, chopped
  coarsely
2 tbsp Thai red curry paste
450 ml/15 fl oz fish stock
2 tbsp fish sauce
2 tbsp Thai soy sauce
6 sprigs fresh Thai basil
400 g/14 oz canned straw
  mushrooms, drained
350 g/12 oz large cooked
  shelled prawns
boiled jasmine rice, to serve

method

Heat the oil in a wok and stir-fry the spring onions and garlic for 2–3 minutes. Add the creamed coconut, red curry paste and fish stock and heat gently until the coconut has dissolved.

Stir in the fish sauce and soy sauce, then add the basil, mushrooms and prawns. Gradually bring to the boil and serve immediately with jasmine rice.

made with vegetables

Thai food is ideal for both strict vegetarians and for those who enjoy their vegetables crisply cooked and bursting with goodness and flavour. A wonderful range of vegetables is grown in Thailand, from aubergine and spring onions to a variety of vibrant greens including pak choi and beans.

Protein in vegetarian dishes is provided by tofu (a nutritious cholesterol-free soybean curd with a bland taste, which readily absorbs flavourings) and nuts such as cashews, making for an exceptionally healthy diet that is low in saturated fats and sodium. As with meat and fish dishes, rice and noodles are a big feature of vegetable-based meals. Noodles come in a variety of shapes and sizes; some are made, rather like pasta, from wheat flour, eggs and water, but noodles made from rice or from ground mung beans have a lighter texture and are ideal for those on a gluten-free diet.

Thai vegetable dishes are undoubtedly perfect for the health-conscious, but they are also delicious, quick and easy to make, and form an essential part of an authentic Thai meal, where they will join a selection of meat- and fish-based dishes. Note that, for strict vegetarians, you should use vegetable rather than chicken stock where relevant, and omit ingredients such as shrimp paste and fish sauce.

aubergine &
bean curry

ingredients

SERVES 4

2 tbsp vegetable or peanut oil

1 onion, chopped

2 garlic cloves, crushed

2 fresh red chillies, deseeded
    and chopped

1 tbsp Thai red curry paste

1 large aubergine, cut into
    chunks

115 g/4 oz pea or small
    aubergines

115 g/4 oz baby broad beans

115 g/4 oz fine green beans

300 ml/10 fl oz vegetable
    stock

55 g/2 oz block creamed
    coconut, chopped

3 tbsp Thai soy sauce

1 tsp jaggery or soft light
    brown sugar

3 kaffir lime leaves, torn
    coarsely

4 tbsp chopped fresh
    coriander

method

Heat the oil in a wok or large frying pan and sauté the onion, garlic and chillies for 1–2 minutes. Stir in the curry paste and cook for 1–2 minutes.

Add the aubergines and cook for 3–4 minutes, until starting to soften. (You may need to add a little more oil as aubergines soak it up quickly.) Add the beans and stir-fry for 2 minutes.

Pour in the stock and add the creamed coconut, soy sauce, sugar and lime leaves. Bring gently to the boil and cook until the coconut has dissolved. Stir in the coriander and serve hot.

aubergine & mushroom stuffed omelette

ingredients

SERVES 4

3 tbsp vegetable oil

1 garlic clove, finely chopped

1 small onion, finely chopped

1 small aubergine, diced

1/2 small green pepper,
    deseeded and chopped

1 large dried shiitake
    mushroom, soaked,
    drained and sliced

1 tomato, diced

1 tbsp light soy sauce

1/2 tsp sugar

1/4 tsp pepper

2 large eggs

salad leaves, tomato wedges
    and cucumber slices, `to
    garnish

dipping sauce, to serve

method

Heat half the oil in a large frying pan. Add the garlic and cook over high heat for 30 seconds. Add the onion and the aubergine and continue to stir-fry until golden.

Add the pepper and stir-fry for a further 1 minute to soften. Stir in the mushroom, tomato, soy sauce, sugar and pepper. Remove from the pan and keep hot.

Beat the eggs together lightly. Heat the remaining oil in a clean frying pan, swirling to coat a wide area. Pour in the egg and swirl to set around the pan.

When the egg is set, spoon the filling into the centre. Fold in the sides of the omelette to form a square package.

Slide the omelette carefully onto a warmed dish and garnish with salad leaves, tomato wedges and cucumber slices. Serve with a dipping sauce.

stuffed aubergines

ingredients

SERVES 4

8 small aubergines

2 tbsp vegetable or peanut oil

4 shallots, chopped finely

2 garlic cloves, crushed

2 fresh red chillies, deseeded
and chopped

1 courgette, chopped
coarsely

115 g/4 oz block creamed
coconut, chopped

few Thai basil leaves, chopped

small handful of fresh
coriander, chopped

4 tbsp Thai soy sauce

rice with chopped spring
onions, to serve

sweet chilli sauce, to serve

method

Put the aubergines in a roasting pan and cook in a
preheated oven, 200°C/400°F/Gas Mark 6, for 8–10
minutes, until just softened. Cut in half and scoop out
the flesh, reserving the shells.

Heat the oil in a wok or large frying pan and sauté the
shallots, garlic and chilli for 2–3 minutes before adding
the courgettes and aubergine flesh. Add the creamed
coconut, herbs and soy sauce and simmer for 3–4
minutes.

Divide the mixture between the aubergine shells.
Return to the oven for 5–10 minutes, until hot, and
serve immediately with rice and sweet chilli sauce.

tofu & green vegetable curry

ingredients

SERVES 4

vegetable oil, for deep-frying

225 g/8 oz firm tofu, cubed

2 tbsp vegetable or peanut oil

1 tbsp chilli oil

2 fresh green chillies, deseeded and sliced

2 garlic cloves, crushed

6 spring onions, sliced

2 medium courgettes, cut into sticks

1/2 cucumber, peeled, deseeded, and sliced

1 green pepper, deseeded and sliced

1 small head of broccoli, cut into florets

55 g/2 oz fine green beans, halved

55 g/2 oz frozen peas, thawed

300 ml/10 fl oz vegetable stock

55 g/2 oz block creamed coconut, chopped

2 tbsp Thai soy sauce

1 tsp soft light brown sugar

4 tbsp chopped fresh parsley

method

Heat the oil for deep-frying in a frying pan and carefully lower in the tofu cubes, in batches, and cook for 2–3 minutes, until golden brown. Remove with a slotted spoon and drain on kitchen paper.

Heat the other oils in a wok and stir-fry the chillies, garlic and spring onions for 2–3 minutes. Add the courgettes, cucumber, green pepper, broccoli and green beans and stir-fry for a further 2–3 minutes.

Add the peas, stock, coconut, soy sauce and sugar. Cover and simmer for 2–3 minutes, until all the vegetables are tender and the coconut has dissolved.

Stir in the tofu and serve immediately, sprinkled with the chopped fresh parsley.

rice noodles with mushrooms & tofu

ingredients

SERVES 4

225 g/8 oz rice stick noodles

2 tbsp vegetable oil

1 garlic clove, finely chopped

2-cm/³/₄-inch piece fresh root
    ginger, finely chopped

4 shallots, thinly sliced

225 g/8 oz sliced shiitake
    mushrooms

100 g/3¹/₂ oz firm tofu (drained
    weight), cut into 1.5-cm/
    ¹/₂-inch dice

2 tbsp light soy sauce

1 tbsp rice wine or dry sherry

1 tbsp Thai fish sauce

1 tbsp smooth peanut butter

1 tsp chilli sauce

2 tbsp toasted peanuts,
    chopped

shredded fresh basil leaves

method

Place the rice noodles in a bowl, then cover with hot water and soak for 15 minutes, or according to the packet directions. Drain well.

Heat the oil in a large frying pan. Add the garlic, ginger and shallots and stir-fry for 1–2 minutes, or until softened and lightly browned.

Add the mushrooms and stir-fry for a further 2–3 minutes. Stir in the tofu and toss gently to brown lightly.

Mix the soy sauce, rice wine, fish sauce, peanut butter and chilli sauce together in a small bowl, then stir into the pan.

Stir in the rice noodles and toss to coat evenly in the sauce. Sprinkle with peanuts and shredded basil leaves and serve hot.

vegetables with tofu & spinach

ingredients

SERVES 4

vegetable or peanut oil, for
    deep-frying
225 g/8 oz firm tofu, drained
    and cut into cubes
2 tbsp vegetable or peanut oil
2 onions, chopped
2 garlic cloves, chopped
1 fresh red chilli, deseeded
    and sliced
3 celery stalks, sliced
    diagonally
225 g/8 oz mushrooms, sliced
    thickly
115 g/4 oz baby corn, cut in
    half
1 red pepper, deseeded and
    cut into strips
3 tbsp Thai red curry paste
400 ml/14 fl oz coconut milk
1 tsp soft light brown sugar
2 tbsp Thai soy sauce
225 g/8 oz baby spinach
    leaves

method

Heat the oil for deep-frying in a frying pan and deep-fry
the tofu cubes, in batches, for 4–5 minutes, until crisp
and browned. Remove with a slotted spoon and drain on
kitchen paper.

Heat 2 tablespoons of the oil in a wok or frying pan and
stir-fry the onions, garlic and chilli for 1–2 minutes, until
they start to soften. Add the celery, mushrooms, baby
corn and red pepper and stir-fry for 3–4 minutes, until
they soften.

Stir in the curry paste and coconut milk and gradually
bring to the boil. Add the sugar and soy sauce and then
the spinach. Cook, stirring constantly, until the spinach
has wilted. Serve immediately, topped with the tofu.

cauliflower & beans with cashews

ingredients

SERVES 4

1 tbsp vegetable or peanut oil

1 tbsp chilli oil

1 onion, chopped

2 garlic cloves, chopped

2 tbsp Thai red curry paste

1 small cauliflower, cut into florets

175 g/6 oz yard-long beans, cut into 7.5-cm/3-inch lengths

150 ml/5 fl oz vegetable stock

2 tbsp Thai soy sauce

50 g/1³/₄ oz toasted cashews, to garnish

method

Heat both the oils in a wok and stir-fry the onion and garlic until softened. Add the curry paste and stir-fry for 1–2 minutes.

Add the cauliflower and beans and stir-fry for 3–4 minutes, until softened. Pour in the stock and soy sauce and simmer for 1–2 minutes. Serve immediately, garnished with the cashews.

spiced cashew nut curry

ingredients

SERVES 4

250 g/8³/₄ oz unsalted cashew
    nuts
1 tsp coriander seeds
1 tsp cumin seeds
2 cardamom pods, crushed
1 tbsp corn oil
1 onion, finely sliced
1 garlic clove, crushed
1 small fresh green chilli,
    deseeded and chopped
1 cinnamon stick
¹/₂ tsp ground turmeric
4 tbsp coconut cream
300 ml/10 fl oz hot vegetable
    stock
3 dried kaffir lime leaves,
    crumbled
coriander leaves, to garnish
freshly cooked jasmine rice,
    to serve

method

Place the cashew nuts in a bowl, then cover with cold water and soak overnight. Drain thoroughly. Crush the seeds and cardamom pods in a mortar using a pestle.

Heat the oil in a large frying pan. Add the onion and garlic and stir-fry for 2–3 minutes to soften but not brown. Add the chilli, crushed spices, cinnamon stick and turmeric and stir-fry for a further 1 minute.

Add the coconut cream and the hot stock to the frying pan. Bring to the boil, then add the cashew nuts and lime leaves.

Cover the pan, then reduce the heat and simmer for 20 minutes. Serve hot with jasmine rice garnished with coriander leaves.

courgette & cashew curry

ingredients

SERVES 4

2 tbsp vegetable or peanut oil
6 spring onions, chopped
2 garlic cloves, chopped
2 fresh green chillies,
     deseeded and chopped
450 g/1 lb courgettes, cut into
     thick slices
115 g/4 oz shiitake
     mushrooms, halved
55 g/2 oz beansprouts
75 g/3 oz cashews, toasted or
     dry-fried
few Chinese chives, chopped
4 tbsp Thai soy sauce
1 tsp fish sauce
rice or noodles, to serve

method

Heat the oil in a wok or large frying pan and sauté the onions, garlic and chillies for 1–2 minutes, until softened but not browned.

Add the courgettes and mushrooms to the wok and cook for 2–3 minutes until tender.

Add the beansprouts, nuts, chives and both sauces and stir-fry for 1–2 minutes.

Serve hot with rice or noodles.

sweet-&-sour vegetables with cashews

ingredients

SERVES 4

1 tbsp vegetable or peanut oil

1 tsp chilli oil

2 onions, sliced

2 carrots, sliced thinly

2 courgettes, sliced thinly

115 g/4 oz broccoli, cut into
   florets

115 g/4 oz white mushrooms,
   sliced

115 g/4 oz small pak choi,
   halved

2 tbsp jaggery or soft light
   brown sugar

2 tbsp Thai soy sauce

1 tbsp rice vinegar

75 g/3 oz cashews

method

Heat both the oils in a wok or frying pan and stir-fry the onions for 1–2 minutes, until they start to soften.

Add the carrots, courgettes and broccoli and stir-fry for 2–3 minutes. Add the mushrooms, pak choi, sugar, soy sauce and rice vinegar and stir-fry for 1–2 minutes.

Meanwhile, dry-fry or toast the cashews. Sprinkle the cashews over the stir-fry and serve immediately.

vegetable & coconut curry

ingredients

SERVES 4

1 kg/2 lb 4 oz mixed
    vegetables
1 onion, coarsely chopped
3 garlic cloves, thinly sliced
2.5-cm/1-inch piece fresh
    root ginger, thinly sliced
2 fresh green chillies,
    deseeded and
    finely chopped
1 tbsp vegetable oil
1 tsp ground turmeric
1 tsp ground coriander
1 tsp ground cumin
200 g/7 oz creamed coconut
600 ml/20 fl oz boiling water
salt and pepper
2 tbsp chopped coriander,
    to garnish
freshly cooked rice, to serve

method

Cut the mixed vegetables into chunks. Place the onion, garlic, ginger and chillies in a food processor and process until almost smooth.

Heat the oil in a large, heavy-based frying pan. Add the onion mixture and cook for 5 minutes.

Add the turmeric, coriander and cumin and cook for 3–4 minutes, stirring. Add the mixed vegetables and stir to coat in the spice paste.

Mix the creamed coconut and boiling water together in a jug. Stir until the coconut has dissolved. Add the coconut milk to the vegetables, then cover and simmer for 30–40 minutes, or until the vegetables are tender.

Season to taste with salt and pepper, then garnish with the chopped coriander and serve with rice.

mixed vegetables with quick-fried basil

ingredients

SERVES 4

2 tbsp vegetable or peanut oil

2 garlic cloves, chopped

1 onion, sliced

115 g/4 oz baby corn, cut in
    half diagonally

1/2 cucumber, peeled, halved,
    deseeded, and sliced

225 g/8 oz canned water
    chestnuts, drained and
    rinsed

60 g/2 oz mangetout, trimmed

115 g/4 oz shiitake
    mushrooms

1 red pepper, deseeded and
    sliced thinly

1 tbsp soft light brown sugar

2 tbsp Thai soy sauce

1 tbsp fish sauce

1 tbsp rice vinegar

boiled rice, to serve

quick-fried basil

vegetable or peanut oil, for
    cooking

8–12 sprigs fresh Thai basil

method

Heat the oil in a wok and stir-fry the garlic and onion for
1–2 minutes. Add the corn, cucumber, water chestnuts,
mangetout, mushrooms and red pepper and stir-fry for
2–3 minutes, until starting to soften.

Add the sugar, soy sauce, fish sauce and vinegar and
gradually bring to the boil. Simmer for 1–2 minutes.

Meanwhile, heat the oil for the basil in a wok or frying
pan and, when hot, add the basil sprigs. Cook for 20–30
seconds, until crisp. Remove with a slotted spoon and
drain thoroughly on kitchen paper.

Garnish the vegetable stir-fry with the crispy basil and
serve immediately, with the boiled rice.

asian vegetables with yellow bean sauce

ingredients

SERVES 4

1 aubergine

salt

2 tbsp vegetable oil

3 garlic cloves, crushed

4 spring onions, chopped

1 small red pepper, deseeded
 and thinly sliced

4 baby corn cobs, halved
 lengthways

115 g/4 oz mangetout

200 g/7 oz green pak choi,
 coarsely shredded

425 g/14½ oz canned straw
 mushrooms, drained

115 g/4 oz beansprouts

2 tbsp rice wine or dry sherry

2 tbsp yellow bean sauce

2 tbsp dark soy sauce

1 tsp chilli sauce

1 tsp sugar

150 ml/5 fl oz vegetable stock

1 tsp cornflour

2 tsp water

method

Cut the aubergine into 5-cm/2-inch long thin sticks. Place in a colander, then sprinkle with salt and let stand for 30 minutes. Rinse in cold water and dry thoroughly with kitchen paper.

Heat the oil in a frying pan or preheated wok. Add the garlic, spring onions and pepper and stir-fry over high heat for 1 minute. Stir in the aubergine pieces and stir-fry for a further 1 minute, or until softened.

Stir in the baby corn cobs and mangetout and stir-fry for 1 minute. Add the pak choi, mushrooms and beansprouts and stir-fry for 30 seconds.

Mix the rice wine, yellow bean sauce, soy sauce, chilli sauce and sugar together in a bowl, then add to the pan with the stock. Bring to the boil, stirring constantly.

Slowly blend the cornflour with the water to form a smooth paste, then stir quickly into the pan and cook for a further minute. Serve immediately.

egg-fried rice with vegetables & crispy onions

ingredients

SERVES 4

4 tbsp vegetable or peanut oil

2 garlic cloves, chopped finely

2 fresh red chillies, deseeded and chopped

115 g/4 oz mushrooms, sliced

55 g/2 oz mangetout, halved

55 g/2 oz baby corn, halved

3 tbsp Thai soy sauce

1 tbsp jaggery or soft light brown sugar

few Thai basil leaves

350 g/12 oz rice, cooked and cooled

2 eggs, beaten

2 onions, sliced

method

Heat half the oil in a wok or large frying pan and sauté the garlic and chillies for 2–3 minutes.

Add the mushrooms, mangetout and baby corn and stir-fry for 2–3 minutes, then add the soy sauce, sugar and basil. Stir in the rice.

Push the mixture to one side of the wok and add the eggs to the bottom. Stir until lightly set before combining into the rice mixture.

Heat the remaining oil in another pan and sauté the onions until crispy and brown. Serve the rice topped with the onions.

potato & spinach yellow curry

ingredients

SERVES 4

2 garlic cloves, finely chopped
3-cm/1¼-inch piece fresh
   galangal, finely chopped
1 lemon grass stem, finely
   chopped
1 tsp coriander seeds
3 tbsp vegetable oil
2 tsp Thai red curry paste
½ tsp ground turmeric
175 ml/6 fl oz coconut milk
250 g/9 oz potatoes, cut into
   2-cm/¾-inch cubes
300 ml/5 fl oz vegetable stock
200 g/7 oz fresh young
   spinach leaves
1 small onion, thinly sliced

method

Place the garlic, galangal, lemon grass and coriander seeds in a mortar and, using a pestle, grind to make a smooth paste.

Heat 2 tablespoons of the oil in a frying pan or preheated wok. Stir in the garlic paste mixture and stir-fry for 30 seconds. Stir in the curry paste and turmeric, then add the coconut milk and bring to the boil.

Add the potatoes and stock. Return to the boil, then reduce the heat and simmer, uncovered, for 10–12 minutes, or until the potatoes are almost tender.

Stir in the spinach and simmer until the leaves are wilted.

Meanwhile, heat the remaining oil in a separate frying pan. Add the onion and cook until crisp and golden brown. Place the crispy fried onions on top of the curry just before serving.

carrot &
pumpkin curry

ingredients

SERVES 4

150 ml/5 fl oz vegetable stock
2.5-cm/1-inch piece fresh
    galangal, sliced
2 garlic cloves, chopped
1 lemon grass stalk (white
    part only), chopped finely
2 fresh red chillies, deseeded
    and chopped
4 carrots, peeled and cut into
    chunks
225 g/8 oz pumpkin, peeled,
    deseeded and cut into
    cubes
2 tbsp vegetable or peanut oil
2 shallots, chopped finely
3 tbsp Thai yellow curry paste
400 ml/14 fl oz coconut milk
4–6 sprigs fresh Thai basil
25 g/1 oz toasted pumpkin
    seeds, to garnish

method

Pour the stock into a large saucepan and bring to the
boil. Add the galangal, half the garlic, the lemon grass
and chillies and simmer for 5 minutes. Add the carrots
and pumpkin and simmer for 5–6 minutes, until tender.

Meanwhile, heat the oil in a wok or frying pan and stir-
fry the shallots and the remaining garlic for 2–3 minutes.
Add the curry paste and stir-fry for 1–2 minutes.

Stir the shallot mixture into the pan and add the coconut
milk and basil. Simmer for 2–3 minutes. Serve hot,
sprinkled with the toasted pumpkin seeds.

stir-fried ginger mushrooms

ingredients

SERVES 4

2 tbsp vegetable oil

3 garlic cloves, crushed

1 tbsp Thai red curry paste

$1/2$ tsp ground turmeric

425 g/15 oz canned straw
    mushrooms, drained and
    halved

2-cm/$3/4$-inch piece fresh root
    ginger, finely shredded

150 ml/5 fl oz coconut milk

40 g/$1^1/2$ oz dried shiitake
    mushrooms, soaked,
    drained and sliced

1 tbsp lemon juice

1 tbsp light soy sauce

2 tsp sugar

$1/2$ tsp salt

8 cherry tomatoes, halved

200 g/7 oz firm tofu

diced coriander leaves, for
    sprinkling

Thai fragrant rice, to serve

spring onion curls, to garnish

method

Heat the oil in a preheated wok or large frying pan.
Add the garlic and cook for 1 minute, stirring. Stir in
the curry paste and turmeric and cook for a further
30 seconds.

Stir in the straw mushrooms and ginger and stir-fry for
2 minutes. Stir in the coconut milk and bring to the boil.

Stir in the shiitake mushrooms, lemon juice, soy sauce,
sugar and salt and heat thoroughly. Add the tomatoes
and tofu and toss gently to heat through.

Sprinkle the coriander over the mixture and serve hot
with freshly cooked fragrant rice garnished with spring
onion curls.

julienne
vegetable salad

ingredients

SERVES 4

4 tbsp vegetable or peanut oil
225 g/8 oz tofu with herbs,
    cubed
1 red onion, sliced
4 spring onions, cut into
    5-cm/2-inch lengths
1 garlic clove, chopped
2 carrots, cut into short,
    thin sticks
115 g/4 oz fine green beans,
    trimmed
1 yellow pepper, deseeded
    and cut into strips
115 g/4 oz head of broccoli,
    cut into florets
1 large courgette, cut into
    short, thin sticks
55 g/2 oz beansprouts
2 tbsp Thai red curry paste
4 tbsp Thai soy sauce
1 tbsp rice wine vinegar
1 tsp soft light brown sugar
few Thai basil leaves
350 g/12 oz rice vermicelli
    noodles

method

Heat the oil in a wok or large frying pan and cook the
tofu cubes for 3–4 minutes, until browned on all sides.
Lift out of the oil and drain on kitchen paper.

Add the onions, garlic and carrots to the hot oil and cook
for 1–2 minutes before adding the rest of the vegetables,
except for the beansprouts. Stir-fry for 2–3 minutes.

Add the beansprouts, then stir in the curry paste, soy,
vinegar, sugar and basil leaves. Cook for 30 seconds.

Soak the noodles in boiling water or stock for 2–3 minutes
(check the packet instructions) or until tender, and drain
well.

Pile the vegetables onto the noodles and serve topped
with the tofu cubes. Garnish with extra basil if desired.

to finish

This chapter on desserts, rather like the appetizers chapter, is something of a departure from authentic Thai culinary tradition, because the Thai people usually finish their meals with nothing more than a basket of their fabulous tropical fruits, such as mangoes, guavas, pineapples and lychees. There are no dairy products in Thailand, so the familiar Western desserts and 'comfort puddings', rich in cream or chocolate, simply do not exist.

The recipes here, therefore, are a combination of dishes using the wonderful, colourful fruits and exotic flavourings of Thailand, such as the Tropical Fruit in Lemon Grass Syrup illustrated here, with a few definite 'cheats' like the Banana & Coconut Ice Cream and the Creamy Mango Brûlée, a marvellous fusion of East and West in one small ramekin.

Coconuts are grown in Thailand and their flesh and 'milk' are used extensively in cooking, forming almost as important a part of the diet as rice. Coconut products are readily available in cans and cartons, but you can use a fresh coconut – if you can get into it. The best way is to hold the coconut over a bowl to catch the milk and, using a hammer, tap around the centre of the shell until it cracks in half.

roasted spicy pineapple

ingredients

SERVES 4

1 pineapple

1 mango, peeled, seeded
    and sliced

55 g/2 oz butter

4 tbsp golden syrup

1–2 tsp cinnamon

1 tsp freshly grated nutmeg

4 tbsp soft brown sugar

2 passion fruit

150 ml/5 fl oz soured cream

finely grated rind of 1 orange

method

Use a sharp knife to cut off the top, base and skin of the
pineapple, then cut into quarters. Remove the central
core and cut the flesh into large cubes. Place the cubes
in a roasting pan with the mango.

Place the butter, syrup, cinnamon, nutmeg and sugar in
a small saucepan and heat gently, stirring constantly, until
melted. Pour the mixture over the fruit. Roast in a
preheated oven, 200°C/400°F/Gas Mark 6, for 20–30
minutes, until the fruit is browned.

Halve the passion fruit and scoop out the seeds. Spoon
over the roasted fruit. Mix the soured cream and orange
rind together and serve with the fruit.

pineapple with cardamom & lime

ingredients

SERVES 4

1 pineapple

2 cardamom pods

thinly pared lime rind

4 tbsp water

1 tbsp brown sugar

3 tbsp lime juice

fresh mint sprigs and
    whipped cream,
    to decorate

method

Cut the top and base from the pineapple, then cut away the peel and remove the 'eyes' from the flesh. Cut into quarters and remove the core. Slice the pineapple lengthways and place in a large serving dish.

Crush the cardamom pods in a mortar using a pestle and place in a saucepan with the lime rind and water. Bring the mixture to the boil, then reduce the heat and simmer for 30 seconds.

Remove the pan from the heat and add the sugar, then cover with a lid and infuse for 5 minutes.

Stir in the sugar to dissolve, add the lime juice, then strain the syrup over the pineapple. Cover and chill in the refrigerator for 30 minutes.

When ready to serve, decorate with mint sprigs and a spoonful of whipped cream.

pineapple &
lime sorbet

ingredients

SERVES 4

225 g/8 oz caster sugar
600 ml/20 fl oz water
grated rind and juice of 2 limes
1 small pineapple, peeled,
    quartered and chopped
sweet biscuits, to serve

method

Put the sugar and water into a saucepan and heat gently, stirring until the sugar has dissolved. Bring to the boil and simmer for 10 minutes.

Stir in the grated rind and half the lime juice. Remove from the heat and let cool.

Put the pineapple in a blender or food processor and process until smooth. Add to the cold syrup with the remaining lime juice. Pour into a freezerproof container and freeze until crystals have formed around the edge.

Turn out the sorbet into a bowl. Beat well with a fork to break up the crystals. Return to the freezer and chill overnight. Serve in scoops with sweet biscuits.

grilled bananas

ingredients

SERVES 4

55 g/2 oz block creamed
 coconut, chopped
150 ml/5 fl oz double cream
4 bananas
juice and rind of 1 lime
1 tbsp vegetable or peanut oil
50 g/1³/₄ oz dry unsweetened
 coconut

method

Put the creamed coconut and double cream in a small saucepan and heat gently until the coconut has dissolved. Remove from the heat and set aside to cool for 10 minutes, then whisk until thick but floppy.

Peel the bananas and toss in the lime juice and rind. Lightly oil a preheated griddle pan and cook the bananas, turning once, for 2–3 minutes, until soft and browned.

Toast the dry unsweetened coconut on a piece of foil under a grill until lightly browned. Serve the bananas with the coconut cream, sprinkled with the toasted coconut.

bananas in coconut milk

ingredients

SERVES 4

4 large bananas

350 ml/12 fl oz coconut milk

2 tbsp caster sugar

pinch of salt

1 tsp orange flower water

1 tbsp shredded fresh mint

2 tbsp cooked mung beans

fresh mint sprigs, to decorate

method

Peel the bananas and cut them into short chunks. Place in a large saucepan with the coconut milk, sugar and salt. Heat gently until boiling and simmer for 1 minute. Remove the pan from the heat.

Sprinkle the orange flower water over the banana mixture. Stir in the mint and spoon into a serving dish.

Place the mung beans in a heavy-based frying pan and cook over high heat until they turn crisp and golden, shaking the pan occasionally. Let the beans cool slightly, then crush lightly in a mortar using a pestle.

Sprinkle the toasted beans over the bananas and serve warm or cold, decorated with mint sprigs.

banana-stuffed crêpes

ingredients

SERVES 4

225 g/8 oz plain flour
2 tbsp soft light brown sugar
2 eggs
450 ml/15 fl oz milk
grated rind and juice of 1 lemon
55 g/2 oz butter
3 bananas
4 tbsp golden syrup

method

Combine the flour and sugar and beat in the eggs and half the milk. Beat together until smooth. Gradually add the remaining milk, stirring constantly to make a smooth batter. Stir in the lemon rind.

Melt a little butter in a 20-cm/8-inch frying pan and pour in one-quarter of the batter. Tilt the pan to coat the bottom and cook for 1–2 minutes, until set. Flip the crêpe over and cook the second side. Slide out of the pan and keep warm. Repeat to make 3 more crêpes.

Slice the bananas and toss in the lemon juice. Pour the syrup over them and toss together. Fold each crêpe in half and then in half again and fill the centre with the banana mixture. Serve warm.

banana & coconut ice cream

ingredients

SERVES 6–8

3 oz/85 g block creamed
     coconut, chopped
600 ml/20 fl oz double cream
225 g/8 oz icing sugar
2 bananas
1 tsp lemon juice
fresh fruit, to serve

method

Put the creamed coconut in a small bowl. Add just enough boiling water to cover and stir until the coconut is dissolved. Let cool.

Whip the cream with the sugar until thick but still floppy. Mash the bananas with the lemon juice and whisk gently into the cream, along with the cold coconut.

Transfer to a freezerproof container and freeze overnight. Serve in scoops with fresh fruit.

mango & lime sorbet

ingredients

SERVES 4

115 g/4 oz caster sugar
150 ml/5 fl oz water
finely grated rind of 3 limes
2 tbsp coconut cream
2 large ripe mangoes
150 ml/5 fl oz lime juice
curls of fresh coconut,
    toasted, to decorate

method

Place the sugar, water and lime rind in a small saucepan and heat gently, stirring constantly, until the sugar dissolves. Boil rapidly for 2 minutes to reduce slightly, then remove the pan from the heat and strain into a heatproof bowl or jug. Stir in the coconut cream and let cool.

Halve the mangoes, then remove the stones and peel thinly. Chop the flesh coarsely and place in a food processor with the lime juice. Process to a smooth purée and transfer to a small bowl.

Pour the cooled syrup into the mango purée, mixing evenly. Tip into a large, freezerproof container and freeze for 1 hour, or until slushy in texture. Alternatively, use an ice cream machine.

Remove the container from the freezer and beat with an electric mixer to break up the ice crystals. Refreeze for a further hour, then remove from the freezer and beat the contents again until smooth.

Cover the container, then return to the freezer and leave until firm. To serve, remove from the freezer and let stand at room temperature for 15 minutes before scooping into individual glass dishes. Sprinkle with toasted coconut to decorate.

creamy mango brûlée

ingredients

SERVES 4

2 mangoes

250 g/9 oz Mascarpone
   cheese

200 ml/7 fl oz Greek-style
   yogurt

1 tsp ground ginger

grated rind and juice of 1 lime

2 tbsp soft light brown sugar

8 tbsp raw brown sugar

method

Slice the mangoes on either side of the stone. Discard
the stone and peel the fruit. Slice and then chop the
fruit. Divide it between 4 ramekins.

Beat the Mascarpone cheese with the yogurt. Fold in the
ginger, lime rind and juice and soft brown sugar. Divide
the mixture between the ramekins and level off the tops.
Chill for 2 hours.

Sprinkle 2 tablespoons of raw brown sugar over the top
of each dish, covering the creamy mixture. Place under
a hot grill for 2–3 minutes, until melted and browned.
Let cool, then chill until needed. This dessert should be
eaten on the day made.

mangoes in lime syrup

ingredients

SERVES 4

2 large ripe mangoes
1 lime
1 lemon grass stem, chopped
3 tbsp caster sugar

method

Halve the mangoes, then remove the stones and peel off the skins.

Slice the flesh into long, thin slices and carefully arrange them in a wide serving dish.

Remove a few shreds of the rind from the lime for decoration, then cut the lime in half and squeeze out the juice.

Place the lime juice in a small saucepan with the lemon grass and sugar. Heat gently without boiling until the sugar is completely dissolved. Remove the pan from the heat and let cool completely.

Strain the cooled syrup into a small jug and pour evenly over the mango slices.

Sprinkle with the lime rind strips. Cover and chill in the refrigerator before serving.

lychee & ginger sorbet

ingredients

SERVES 4

800 g/1 lb 12 oz canned
    lychees in syrup
finely grated rind of 1 lime
2 tbsp lime juice
3 tbsp preserved ginger syrup
2 egg whites
star fruit slices and slivers of
    preserved ginger,
    to decorate

method

Drain the lychees, reserving the syrup. Place the lychees in a food processor or blender with the lime rind, juice and preserved ginger syrup and process until completely smooth. Transfer to a large bowl.

Mix the purée thoroughly with the reserved lychee syrup, then pour into a large, freezerproof container and freeze for 1–1½ hours, or until slushy in texture. Alternatively, use an ice cream machine.

Remove from the freezer and whisk to break up the ice crystals. Whisk the egg whites in a clean, dry bowl until stiff, then quickly and lightly fold into the ice mixture.

Return to the freezer and leave until firm. Serve the sorbet in scoops, with slices of star fruit and preserved ginger to decorate.

mixed fruit salad

ingredients

SERVES 4

1 papaya, halved, peeled,
  and deseeded

2 bananas, sliced thickly

1 small pineapple, peeled,
  halved, cored and sliced

12 lychees, peeled if fresh

1 small melon, deseeded and
  cut into thin wedges

2 oranges

grated rind and juice of 1 lime

2 tbsp caster sugar

method

Arrange the papaya, bananas, pineapple, lychees and melon on a serving platter. Cut off the rind and pith from the oranges. Cut the orange slices out from between the membranes and add to the fruit platter. Grate a small quantity of the discarded orange rind and add to the platter.

Combine the lime rind and juice and the sugar. Pour over the salad and serve.

tropical fruit in lemon grass syrup

ingredients

SERVES 4

1 honeydew melon

1 small pineapple

1 papaya

400 g/14 oz lychees, pitted

3 passion fruit

1 tbsp grated lime rind and
small handful of fresh mint
leaves, to decorate

lemon grass syrup

85 g/3 oz caster sugar

150 ml/5 fl oz water

2 lemon grass stems, bruised

2 fresh kaffir lime leaves

juice of 1 lime

method

To make the syrup, place all the ingredients in a saucepan. Heat gently until the sugar has dissolved. Bring to the boil and cook, uncovered, for 5 minutes. Let stand overnight.

Cut the melon in half, then remove the seeds and scoop out the flesh with a melon baller. Place in a bowl. Peel the pineapple, cut into quarters lengthways and remove the core. Cut into cubes and add to the melon. Peel the papaya, then remove the seeds, cut the flesh into cubes and add to the other fruits.

Add the lychees. Cut the passion fruit in half and scoop the pulp and seeds into the bowl of fruits. Stir to mix, then transfer to a serving bowl. Remove the lemon grass and lime leaves from the syrup and pour over the fruits. Decorate with the lime rind and mint leaves and serve.

spicy rice pudding

ingredients

SERVES 4

400 ml/14 fl oz canned
    coconut milk
150 ml/5 fl oz milk
55 g/2 oz light soft brown
    sugar
55 g/2 oz short-grain rice
2 tsp allspice
1 oz butter
1 tsp ground cinnamon

method

Put the coconut milk and milk in a saucepan and heat gently. Add the sugar and stir until it has dissolved.

Add the rice and spice and gradually bring to the boil. Simmer gently, stirring frequently, for 45–60 minutes, until thickened.

Stir in the butter and, once it has melted, serve immediately, sprinkled with cinnamon.

coconut cake with lime & ginger syrup

ingredients

SERVES 4

2 large eggs, separated

pinch of salt

55 g/2 oz caster sugar

5 tbsp butter, melted
    and cooled

5 tbsp coconut milk

115 g/4 oz self-rising flour

1/2 tsp baking powder

3 tbsp dry unsweetened
    coconut

4 tbsp preserved ginger syrup

3 tbsp lime juice

to decorate

3 pieces preserved ginger

curls of fresh coconut

finely grated lime rind

method

Cut a 28-cm/11-inch circle of baking parchment and press into an 18-cm/7-inch steamer basket to line it.

Whisk the egg whites with the salt in a clean, dry bowl until stiff. Gradually whisk in the sugar, 1 tablespoon at a time, whisking hard after each addition until the mixture forms stiff peaks.

Whisk in the yolks, then quickly stir in the butter and coconut milk. Sift the flour and baking powder over the mixture, then fold in lightly and evenly with a large metal spoon. Fold in the coconut.

Spoon the mixture into the lined steamer basket and tuck the spare paper over the top. Place the basket over boiling water, then cover and steam for 30 minutes.

Transfer the cake to a plate, remove the paper and let cool slightly. Mix the ginger syrup and lime juice together and spoon over the cake. Cut into squares and decorate with pieces of preserved ginger, curls of coconut and lime rind.